SOUTH SOLO

KAYAKING TO SAVE
THE ALBATROSS

HAYLEY SHEPHARD

Foreword by
BRIAN KEATING

May 26th 2012

Dear Janice & Art,

Here's to the wonderful world of the wild and to all of us who appreciate all of it.

Thanks for your ongoing interest & support.

much love

Hayley

x

BAYEUX

SOUTH SOLO: KAYAKING TO SAVE THE ALBATROSS
© Copyright 2011 Bayeux Arts, Inc. and Hayley Shephard

Unless otherwise noted, photographs are courtesy of and copyright by the photographers – Brandon Harvey ('Curious elephant seal' and 'King penguin on top of the world') and Beth-Anne Masselink ('Our aquatic escort' and 'Peales dolphin near the Falkland Islands'). All other photographs are copyright by Hayley Shephard.

The concept for the three maps and Image Support - Dean Laar

Published by
Bayeux Arts, Inc.
119 Stratton Crescent SW,
Calgary, Canada T3H 1T7

www.bayeux.com
First printing: November 2011

Cover and Book design: PreMediaGlobal

Library and Archives Canada Cataloguing in Publication

Shephard, Hayley
    South solo : kayaking to save the albatross / Hayley Shephard.

Issued also in electronic format.
ISBN 978-1-897411-33-9

    1. Shephard, Hayley—Travel—South Georgia and South Sandwich Islands—South Georgia. 2. Kayaking—South Georgia and South Sandwich Islands—South Georgia. 3. Albatrosses—Conservation—South Georgia and South Sandwich Islands—South Georgia. 4. South Georgia (South Georgia and South Sandwich Islands)—Description and travel. I. Title.

GV776.8835.S68S54 2011   797.122'4099712   C2011-906366-2

Shephard, Hayley
    South solo [electronic resource] : kayaking to save the albatross / Hayley Shephard.

Electronic monograph in EPUB format.
Issued also in print format.
ISBN 978-1-897411-58-2

GV776.8835.S68S54 2011a   797.122'4099712   C2011-906367-0

Printed in Canada

Books published by Bayeux Arts are available at special quantity discounts to use in premiums and sales promotions, or for use in corporate training programs. For more information, please write to Special Sales, Bayeux Arts, Inc., 119 Stratton Crescent SW, Calgary, Canada T3H 1T7.

The ongoing publishing activities of Bayeux Arts, under its "Bayeux" and "Gondolier" imprints, are supported by the Canada Council for the Arts, the Government of Alberta, Alberta Multimedia Development Fund, and the Government of Canada through the Book Publishing Industry Development Program.

 Canada Council Conseil des Arts
for the Arts du Canada

 Government of Alberta ■

 LIVRES CANADA BOOKS

To my mum and dad,

for giving me the freedom to be me, despite the risks and fears, and for supporting all my venturesome endeavours. You took me to the ocean, we camped by a river and you led me through forested trails, and Mother Nature took over from there. I am forever grateful.

We are all genuinely inspired by the wonders of our natural world and the beauty it beholds. It is amongst the trees, by the sea, on a mountain peak and while sharing space with other creatures, where we recognize our authentic connection not only to our Mother Earth but also to ourselves, the human spirit. Visit with nature, listen to her breath and watch as she reveals the precious gifts we were all born to notice.

Hayley

Contents

Foreword

By Brian Keating

What is it in us, this desire to read about extreme adventures that others have endured. Is it the close calls with disaster, the intense visceral disappointment of ambitions not met, or the sheer joy of sweet success? Or is it the delight of living life to the fullest in the presence of the sheer rugged beauty of distant lands, of romantic notions of discovery, or the chance of exquisite wildlife spectacles?

I have met so many of the hardcore modern 'adventurists', those people who make a living out of selling their stories, who have tended to be individuals on 'inward' journeys, so often accomplished for personal and perhaps selfish reasons. There is no question that these extreme journeys require, as a major qualification, a singleness of mind to reach success, but Hayley's journey stands out differently. Very differently.

Self-reliant: yes; single minded: no doubt; strong, skilled and confident: without question. But hers is a larger goal, and one I wholeheartedly endorse. This larger quest is such a noble cause, and is one we all must undertake, eventually, as a way of life. This is the *conservation* cause.

There is a catastrophe descending upon us globally, and too few are taking part in the attempt to slow it, halt it, or even talk about it. It's no secret that wild places and the wild creatures that inhabit these wild spaces need our help. Nature colours the world with intrigue, diversity, inspiration, and simply joy. Ultimately, its healthy function is what sustains all life, including our own.

I have worked in the world of wildlife conservation for 30 years, but my interest in nature has been a part of my own spirit and soul since age 12, when I received my first pair of second- hand binoculars. It was then that I discovered magic. The glint in the robin's eye as it hopped across my suburban lawn, the impossible colouration of a tanager in my neighbourhood forest, my first sighting of a falcon's attempt to secure a kill. These were powerful first-hand observations I made as a young, budding naturalist, events I clearly remember to this day. And Hayley not only witnessed this natural dynamic head-on, but her efforts were for a higher cause: the Albatross. This was Hayley's magic, her passion, her symbol and perhaps personal justification for her inner need to attempt such a dramatic adventure.

Hayley, you embody the spirit that so few possess today. Your sense of discovery and adventure is palpable with every one of your carefully articulated paragraphs. I can't imagine a Southern Ocean without the albatross. What a sad place that would be. Your dedication to such an important cause is only overshadowed by your courage, skill, and perseverance. Thank you for your dogged determination to ensure such an important message is told to a world that needs to hear and understand it. Your voice now comes with the authority of having been there, in the violent, heaving surf.

You have seen the albatross in full flight like few have witnessed, with salt in your teeth, paddling directly into the numbing winds of the Southern Ocean, at kayak level. I cannot think of a better spokesperson for all things wild, because you, Hayley, in your own intimate way, have flown with the albatross.

Dr. Brian Keating worked with the Calgary Zoological Society for three decades, and was the founder of their Conservation Outreach programs, taking him to all 7 continents. He now freelances as a guide, professional speaker, broadcaster, and author. He met Hayley Shephard in the Antarctic, as they worked together on a Russian ice-reinforced ship, when she was formulating her South Georgia circumnavigation plans.

Chapter 1

A Dream is Born

Iaimed my five-metre zodiac for the shore, wishing I had some passengers to hold the craft steady. I desperately needed ballast.[1] With my own weight and a forty-horsepower outboard engine hanging from the stern, plus an empty fuel tank and a light barrel of emergency items stowed in the bow, my zodiac[2] reared up like a spirited mare every time a gust of wind arrived head-on. The katabatic winds[3] came down from the valley which cradled the beach I was heading for.

The wind gathered speed as it raced out to sea, shaking everything in its path. A dark shadow brushed the ocean surface and moved towards me, and I knew a gust of wind was about to hit. In bracing for this and every gust, I slowed down my speed which lowered the bow. I crouched low in the boat, hanging on tight to the safety lines. Then suddenly an even stronger gust hit, taking me by surprise. The dark water seemed to envelop me. The fierce wind lifted my bow straight up towards the sky, and I felt my body falling backwards as the weight of the engine supported the momentum. The bow rose high and I couldn't even see the sky. It seemed that my zodiac was about to be flipped completely upside down. All I could do in trying to stay upright was to steer the bow away from the wind by pushing the tiller hard over towards the right. The zodiac responded; the bow quivered then lowered, settling once again on the water.

---

[1] Weight in the lower portion of a boat, used to add stability.

[2] The zodiac is a brand name for an inflatable motorized boat

[3] A wind that carries high density air from higher elevation down a slope under the force of gravity.

That was too close, I thought, as the adrenaline still pumped through my body. Ending up in these frigid polar seas would be a dangerous outcome I earnestly wished to avoid. How could anyone rescue me when they too would be driving in these conditions and that is only if I were able to hail them on my handheld radio?

Every gust that followed had the same force and, in anticipation of its awesome power, I now turned my zodiac around and reversed, with the greatest weight bearing into the wind. It was a cautionary move, but a necessary one, which made for a slow trip to shore. I was picking up the last of our passengers. I was glad this would be my final trip to shore.

How quickly the weather changed from when we had arrived in South Georgia earlier that morning. It was my first time here and, during our landing, I romanced about the idea of kayaking around the island. I was quick to dream. In the course of a single day, I had seen the many faces of this sub-Antarctic island. It didn't take long for the island to capture my total imagination and I clung to its beauty like a needy child clinging to its mother.

We had approached South Georgia from the open Atlantic, arriving on a Russian ice-strengthened passenger ship after spending three days at sea. As we drew nearer in search of an anchorage, the mountains seemed to grow steeper. Their snow-clad peaks pierced into the storm cloud skies above. Glacial valleys steered their way towards the sea from the rugged interior. And the ice – once part of the land, now floating freely beneath the towering cliffs – was beautiful to behold, but a formidable navigational hazard. The coast was fringed with white water as waves, an offspring of past storms, crashed relentlessly on the shore. The entire scene was foreboding and, in some ways, the island took on an almost inhospitable demeanour. Yet, at the same time the drama, ruggedness, and the security of land beckoned us closer.

Dressed in multiple layers of down and Gore-Tex, we sat in an inflatable rubber dinghy and approached a large, half-moon shaped beach overflowing with wildlife. We were about to land at Salisbury Plain, a beach famous for its abundance of wildlife, including a penguin rookery consisting of 500,000 king penguins. From a mile away, we could hear the trumpeting chorus of penguins and the whimpering squeals from juvenile fur seals, their scattered presence stretching for miles. One particular animal stood out among the rest, perhaps because of its size. It was the 5000 kg southern elephant seal. These blubbery beasts lay sprawled along every section of beach, their bodies jammed side by side, some on top and others underneath. Guttural croaks and growls came from deep within their diaphragm and, with every breath, they released dense condensation which rose like a plume and lingered in the polar air.

We came ashore and meandered through the jam-packed penguin rookery, keeping our distance from the newly hatched penguin chicks. King penguin adults gathered in large numbers, either preening themselves or flirting as they strutted by clusters of potential mates. My aim was to reach the top of a valley, above the river that wove its way from deep within a mountain-claimed glacier. Penguins laced both sides of the river, keeping cool on this unusually calm and sunny day. I found a perfect perching rock and, after checking it for guano and finding it clear, I sat down and looked beyond the rookery and out to sea.

The nearest landmass from where I sat was the now-familiar Falkland Islands, 1400 km away. A vast ocean filled the massive space that separated us. I had never placed myself so far removed from civilization and in a place so remote. The abundance of wildlife swept away any feelings of loneliness. It was a symphony of unrestrained sounds as glaciers cracked and snapped, releasing ancient ice that went tumbling into the sea. The tussock grass, only ankle high, was whipped vigorously by the blowing wind. Antarctic skuas protested loudly as their attempt to snatch a penguin egg from a protective parent was foiled. King penguin parents returned from foraging at sea, their bellies so full and protruding they found it difficult to move themselves from the surf zone. With land under foot, all they needed to do was scurry up the beach before the next wave knocked them off their feet. Due to their protruding bellies, scurrying wasn't an option; instead they stumbled, fell back on their bellies and drifted back out to sea with the outgoing surge. Within the heart of the rookery, parents searched for their chicks and chicks eagerly called out for their parents. With numberless pairs in search of each other, the cacophonic chaos echoed through the valley, filling every nook and cranny of this Antarctic Serengeti.

From the perspective of a kayaker and a nature enthusiast, South Georgia is pure paradise. The coastline is full of character, taking one from the sublime to the treacherous with each paddle stroke. Within the constantly changing scenery the relationship between land and sea tests one's skills and patience. Landing in surf is frequent and the surface on which one lands is as unpredictable as the weather: sand, pebbles, boulders of enormous size and the chance one may stumble upon the infamous tussock mounds. The sunsets and cloud formations are like nothing I have seen anywhere else on the planet. Lenticular[4] clouds are South Georgia's signature, as is the descending sun that spreads fire in the sky using the storm clouds which constantly hover over mountain tops. The ever-changing weather keeps one on one's toes and alert in order to respond to the unexpected fluctuations. There are so few humans that stumbling upon another person is unlikely, unless they too braved the Southern Ocean, which likes to invite the bold and experienced.

The drama of South Georgia is endless. Detached from any land mass or continent, it stands alone with the ruthless wind as a constant companion. Despite its savage reputation, treasures are bountiful. The abundance of wildlife and its indomitable nature captivates and humbles every visitor. Like an ancient tomb or a precious jewel, the island seems somewhat untouchable. It seems to be a sacred land that requires your full attention and stirs you intensely upon your arrival.

---

[4]Having the shape of a double-convex lens.

It was like no other place I had ever had the privilege to explore. On that first day I was not only drawn to its beauty but also felt myself a prisoner to its sheer physical supremacy. It acted like a magnet, drawing me to its heart, never to be parted. From that moment I felt obsessed by South Georgia. It was like risking one's heart, risking everything, when committed to a perilous lover; I was prepared to ignore all dangers. "I want to kayak around this entire island," I announced loudly. "And I want to do it alone."

During my final zodiac ride back to the ship, with passengers whose wide-open eyes reflected their concern as we slowly climbed up each wave and plummeted down, I asked myself, "Am I crazy? What on earth was I thinking? This place is bloody treacherous!" Still, a dream was born that day.

Chapter 2

Back to the Beginning

I clung to the edge of the Olympic-size pool, my legs and feet rotating like a bicycle cog in an attempt to take some pressure off of my white-knuckled grip as I tried to keep my head above water. Hand over hand, I inched my way towards the shallow end of the pool, feeling relief as my feet touched solid concrete below. I turned and looked across the other side of the pool at the deep end where I dared not go. My dad was playfully flicking my sister Naomi up into the air, and as she landed with a lively splash, she giggled. I felt desperately left out of all the fun and games but I was overcome with fear every time I ventured away from the edge of the pool. Dad swam over towards me. "Come on Hayley, don't be a chicken," he called out in jest. "I don't want to," I shouted angrily. "Leave me alone." I felt like a chicken. I felt quite stupid really, being too scared to let go of the edge. At the age of three I was terrified of water.

Eight years later, I sat in an open canoe behind my stepbrother Mike. We were paddling on the Waikato River[5] in a newly purchased canoe while the rest of the family sat at the edge of the river, eagerly watching. We were up river from the family, drifting steadily downstream. Did we have a plan? No, not really. We aimed to start here and end in the calm rapid-free water right in front of where the family sat.

It did not take long for the current to gather strength. Upon noticing this change, we paddled more vigorously,

---

[5]The Waikato River, the longest in New Zealand, is located in central North Island, rising on the slopes of Mount Ruapehu in Tongariro National Park.

trying to steer our way towards an eddy where the water had lost all its speed. We missed the eddy completely and drifted helplessly into the main rapid chain where the waves bucked and the water churned. We noticed a bend in the river and watched how the white water was gathering speed then smashing itself against a steep river wall. At the bend and below the wall was an overhang and, to our disbelief, we were heading straight toward it. As the water took complete control of us, we hung on tightly to the canoe railing. I closed my eyes and screamed and could hear Mike shouting behind me. The rush was unbelievable as we gathered momentum and plunged forward towards what we immediately recognized as danger. To our surprise, the water acted like a suction cushion against the rock wall and held us there for what seemed like minutes, but keeping us up right and clear of the overhang. Eventually the river's powerful grasp released us as the hull of our canoe nestled back on the main rapid. We eased past the wall, clearing it by inches. The lips of frisky waves steepened and splashed forcefully against our bow, drenching our faces and upper body. We cleared our eyes and were relieved to be heading for calmer water. The rapid decelerated into a lethargic pace and we started paddling towards shore. The adrenaline now subsided, we grinned from ear to ear as we made our way towards the beach where our family sat. We were curious to see if anyone had been watching us. "Wow, I thought you kids were toast," Dad announced nervously. "That was pretty close," he added.

After a quick lunch, all we could think about was heading back up and running that section of river again. At the time neither Mike nor I was aware of the potential dangers we had faced during that wild ride down a raging rapid on the Waikato River. I had grown out of my fear of water.

My mum had a fear of water. Growing up she didn't have the opportunity to go to swimming lessons; she could not swim to save us or herself. Both my parents decided to put my sister and me into swimming lessons at an early age. I cannot recall the day or the moment I overcame my fear. All I remember was my unwillingness to get out of the water once

I was in, whether it was in the swimming pool, river or ocean. During watersports day at school, I won every swimming race I entered and quite happily jumped off a ten -metre-high bridge into a deep river below for recreation. One thing about growing up in New Zealand, you are surrounded by water wherever you go and wherever you live. It was the perfect playground.

Growing up I excelled in sports, whether it was badminton, soccer or cross-country running. I was extremely competitive, very motivated and I hated to lose. Inside the classroom I was an average student who put minimal effort into most of the subjects I took in school. "If Hayley were to apply herself and put in more effort, she would do better; she has so much potential," I always read on my school reports.

My mentors were my physical education teachers and sports coaches. My heroes were top New Zealand outdoors people like the sailor Sir Peter Blake and the mountain climber Sir Edmund Hillary. And it was a two-week extensive camp at the Sir Edmund Hillary Outdoor Pursuits Centre of New Zealand that set me on a path towards loving and working and living in the outdoors.

As a little girl it was clear to my parents that I would be able to look after myself. I was fiercely independent and determined to have things go my way, insisting on having the last word in all discussions and arguments. My father described me as self-willed; my mother, as stubborn. In retrospect, it wasn't always easy being the parent who raised me.

As I grew older my father observed the development of my empathy for those less advantaged by physical, mental or cultural differences. I was friends with the nerds, the geeks and the loners as well as those in the 'in' crowd. Little did I know then that my compassion would evolve towards our natural world and become the driving force behind my goals and interest in becoming a dedicated steward of our planet?

I disliked mathematics. It was a subject I continually struggled with; however, the children in my class loved it. I suppose it helps when the teacher takes math outside the classroom. At age twenty one, I successfully completed a teaching diploma and became a middle school teacher, working with children aged eleven to thirteen. Even as a teacher I was very much focused on the outdoors. I certainly followed the specified curriculum but I did it the way I believed was best for the children. It made more sense to approach subjects in a practical and hands-on kind of way, where students see purpose and can connect a task to the reality of their own world. I believe it is important that kids have an understanding of what it is they are trying to learn and to see the purpose.

Writing classes were held beneath the grandmother rimu[6] tree, calculations and measurements were done on the net-ball court and music classes were held along a forested hiking trail. There is nothing quite like a chorus of songbirds in a New Zealand native forest. My passion was taking kids out of the classroom, giving them opportunities to explore the natural world and discover themselves. I organized and ran week-long school camps, after school mountain biking, weekend kayaking adventures for kids. I believed the outdoors, nature and activities within this environment simply brought out the best in kids. I found it gratifying to watch transformations taking place. The geeks became heroes, the loners became leaders, the troublemakers became concerned for the geeks' well-being and the 'in crowd' kids were humbled by the talent and courage of others. It was magic to watch.

---

[6]One of the main evergreen forest trees of New Zealand, the rimu tree can live for as long as 800 years. The small fleshy seed capsules are eaten by both birds and terrestrial rodents that spread the seed across the landscape. The extent of rimu forests is diminishing because of logging and seed destruction by non-native animals.

Chapter 3

Extending My Classroom

After three years teaching in New Zealand, I decided it was time to explore beyond the beautiful shores of my homeland. My journey began in England, where my parents were born and raised and every relative I have lives. It was here the gates to new horizons were opened, expanding my world and amplifying my curiosity. While working in London as a substitute teacher, I maximized my vacation time which took me to countries rich in culture, such as Africa, Nepal, Israel and Jordan. The unique scenery, unusual wildlife, foreign language and unfamiliar food fascinated me. I discovered my attraction towards travelling alone; the enforced self-reliance when having to face challenges and make decisions with only myself to rely on. It seemed to intensify my experience and place more value on the travelling I was doing which I liked very much.

Hanson Island, in British Columbia, Canada, was an unexpected bonus, an accidental adventure. I was visiting my boyfriend at the time, who was a kayak guide. I met him in New Zealand before I had left to travel and back then he told me of his experiences kayaking with killer whales. He showed me the nautical charts of the areas he had kayaked and the beaches he had camped on. He played recorded vocalizations of killer whales and showed me images of the family groups of orca that spend the summer and fall travelling the local waters and feasting on salmon. Back then I was hooked on a region that was 8000 nautical miles away from where I was in New Zealand. In 2003, on a three week vacation I journeyed to Canada and closed in on those 8000 miles. I saw, heard and experienced the whales with my own eyes and ears and I have lived there ever since. I felt transformed the moment I set foot on Hanson Island.

OrcaLab is situated on Hanson Island in Northern Vancouver Island along the Inside Passage. It is a land-based whale research station studying the movements and vocalizations of northern resident orca who return to those waters every summer, foraging for salmon and socializing within their family groups. Paul Spong and Helena Symonds have lived and operated OrcaLab since the early 1970s. I signed up for a volunteer position to assist in the study and to help with the chores of keeping a research camp running. During my two months on Hanson Island, I felt more at home and more myself than I had ever felt before. "So this is what makes me tick," I remember saying to myself.

For two months I slept in a tent that was pitched along the edge of the forest overlooking a bay that led to a passage where orcas passed frequently. Night and day we were gifted by their presence, alerted by the sounds of their blows and calls that were amplified throughout the forest from underwater microphones and mounted outdoor speakers. Living on an island with no roads, a boat as the only means of transport, no electricity, a wood stove for cooking, candle light for reading and water collected from the nearby stream, all brought out the best in me. We were all there for one purpose; to live as a community on Hanson Island, working together, participating in the long-term study of the orca. And all the while our research was conducted in a manner that caused no interference with the whales themselves. Here on Hanson Island I felt like I was truly at home, living my dreams and being myself more truthfully than ever before.

My volunteer work on Hanson Island opened up doors for other whale viewing opportunities. I was asked to guide a kayaking trip in the Johnston Strait area for a commercial kayaking company. With twelve guests, three guides, and nine kayaks (mostly doubles) loaded with camping gear, food and cooking equipment, we embarked on a six day journey which would remove us away from computers, cellphones and cities, placing us in an aquatic and forested setting. For six days and six nights we never once stepped 'indoors.' We slept under canvas, dined beside a well-stoked fire, travelled by kayak propelled only by our own efforts and we frequently interacted with wildlife. As families of orca cruised along the same coastline we travelled, we were often in their company. While sitting onshore, their blows could be heard from a mile away. The waters of the Inside Passage were often pierced by dorsal fins which rose from the depths below as the family groups broke the surface to breathe.

One evening, just before everyone had gone to bed, we heard blows very close to the bay where we were camped. Using flashlights we carefully made our way to the outcrop of rocks which jutted out into the Johnston Strait. The whales were hugging the shore, and when they passed by, we were looking directly down on them. It was a dark night. As they swam by, their movements disturbed the microorganisms which had been charged by the sun all day. The whales were lit up by the bioluminescence which surrounded their bodies like a glowing cape. Later that night, once nestled in our sleeping bags, the sounds of whale blows could be heard from all the way across the Strait. Their sounds carried over the waves by the gentle breeze that, at other times, might carry the scent of forests out to sea.

After guiding this one trip, I worked towards becoming an official kayak guide and found guiding work in Baja, Mexico. About two thirds down the Baja Peninsula is the picturesque town of Loreto. Although it is a small town compared to Cabo San Lucas in the south, international flights from the United States fly into Loreto. For kayakers, the small islands off Loreto are easily accessible and provide the best sample of a Mexican wilderness.

On a typical six day trip, we guided vacationers around the shores of two Islands, Isla Danzante and Isla Carmen, snorkeling beside our lunch beaches and taking walks along the cactus-lined ridges that rose from the beaches. Blows from the largest whales in the world, the Blue and Fin could be heard from faraway, as they foraged along the underwater valley which was teeming with their favorite food, crustaceans. Common and bottlenose dolphins frolicked in the waters right beside our campsites, performing gregarious acrobatics as though trying to get our attention.

We awakened with the sun which also dictated our time to head to bed. The inviting cobalt sea was our pathway and in the midday heat, it was our refreshing sanctuary which gave us the chance to explore the underwater world made up of tropical fish and delectable coral. All of the guides and most of our guests never bothered pitching their tent; instead they slept under the stars. The warm and clear nights made sleeping in a tent unnecessary.

During those years of full-time guiding, it was likely that I slept outside more than I did in. I sat in a kayak seat more than I did in a chair and I probably drove a boat more frequently than I drove a car. The highlight of my years spent living and working beside the sea was the numerous encounters I had with whales. Their blows were constant and in perfect rhythm, like the sound of the sea lapping on a distant shore. They are the largest creatures in the world, feeding on the smallest microorganism. Each specie shares the abundance of the sea, including the path along which they travel. It often seems to me that they are well ahead of human society when it comes to living in harmony with each other and with nature.

Chapter 4

Saving Whales

On December 11th 1969, ten days before I was born, a four-year-old female Orca from the northern resident community of killer whales was swimming alongside her mother during the night of a fierce and terrible storm. They were travelling with other pods which chose that evening to enter Pender Harbour on the Sunshine Coast, north of Vancouver, British Columbia. Their search for protection came to a sudden halt as a fleet of large fishing boats surrounded the whales. Their intention was to take captives. After ten hours of battle twelve whales were taken captive. One of the captives was a four-year-old daughter named Corky. She was a member of the A5 pod. Corky's mother was in her prime and a mother of three offspring. Resident killer whales spend their entire lives together as a family. The only cause for separation is death or captivity. At the time of her capture, Corky was not aware that she would spend the rest of her life separated from her family, living in a small, enclosed concrete tank in SeaWorld, San Diego.

Throughout her years as a captive whale, Corky gave birth to six calves. Every single one died soon after it was born. She has become the longest living captive whale in the world and every day as she jumps through hoops to entertain the crowds, she symbolizes all that is unethical with the human race. The exploitation of animals by human beings for the sake of entertainment is disgraceful. Yet even today, we still tear animals away from their families, remove them from the wild and cage them up for our own enjoyment as though they are our property and it is our right to deal with them as we wish.

In the year 1996, twenty-six years after Corky's capture, I sat in a San Diego hotel for six hours at a sewing machine. This was not my usual choice of activities. I never took to sewing at school; I always had to unpick my work, having done it rather carelessly. This time was different. I had a purpose, an important task that needed to be done and I was motivated.

I was sewing together thousands of square pieces of material two feet by two feet; each square had an image on the fabric drawn with paints, pastels or crayons. Along with the image were messages, 'Give Corky Back,' 'Captivity Kills – Freedom Gives Life' and 'Corky belongs in the wild with her family.' Thousands of children and adults from twenty-two countries were taking part in creating the longest banner in the world which was to be displayed around the entire property of the San Diego SeaWorld where Corky was held captive. I had just returned from New Zealand with two large duffel bags filled with squares designed by New Zealand children that needed sewing together. As I picked up the individual squares and joined them, I read each message and was moved by the words and wisdom of the children of our world. Hour after hour as I sewed the squares together, my skill, motivation and belief in what we as a group were doing grew stronger.

It was a peaceful protest. But on that same day, Corky was not at peace. At approximately midday, a trainer observed Corky speed-swimming around her shallow tank and despite the staff's efforts to calm her, she would not listen and would not slow down. For her safety, they released her into the show-tank which is much deeper. Corky, the longest living captive whale was always known as the co-operative one, their top performer. Corky, on the day of the protest, refused to perform.

Corky remains alive to this day, swimming in her fifteen foot tank, performing to crowds, begging for fish and still speaking the dialect she learned from her mother. Corky is haunted by her own vocalizations as they rebound back from the concrete walls that imprison them instead of echoing throughout the Inside Passage of Vancouver Island, reaching her mother and hearing her mother's voice in response. Within the realm of an orca's world, sound and vibrations are essential. Their dialect is a vital component for communicating. It is how they socialize and keep connected. It is the way the young calves learn from their elders.

The Makah protest of December 1998 was of a different kind. We were angry and appalled at the Washington Coast First Nation tribe, the Makah, and their plans to re-establish their traditional right to hunt whales. They were targeting grey whales and it was for commercial gain. The intended hunt had nothing to do with tradition. The Makah elders even spoke out against the whaling and the intended actions of their younger people, knowing it was wrong and contrary to their traditional and spiritual beliefs.

I was working as a naturalist and zodiac driver for a whale-watching company out of Victoria at the time. Every day we would take boatloads of passengers out to see the southern resident orca. At times we would also encounter humpback whales and on occasion, a grey whale. Season after season the whales had given joy to us and it was our turn to support the whales and give back. The whale-watching community came together to try and put a stop to the intended whale hunt.

I remember standing on the bow of a fifty-foot aluminum boat, a megaphone held to my mouth. "50-calibre rifles and a 150-horsepowered motorboat, where is the tradition in that?" I shouted to the Makah protesters on the shores of Neah Bay in Washington State.

The grey whale has been described as the friendly whale, the people's whale. They are known to approach vessels, even rub alongside the hull in hope of a human hand reaching down to touch them. They are an easy target, unafraid of boats and curious towards humans. I was one of the first proud members of the West Coast Anti-Whaling Society.

Our main objective was to educate the public in the true facts behind the Makah hunting issue and to prevent grey whales from being killed.

Having successfully prevented whales from being killed, we could claim our efforts paid off in that first year. The following year, in May 1999, a three-year-old grey whale was shot and killed by the Makah people. After the whale was towed ashore behind a speedboat and dragged onto land, a Makah member jumped on the dead whale's back and raised his hands in the air. In one hand he held his rifle and he yelled "yahoo" in triumph. Shortly after, all the Makah hunters rushed off to the bar to celebrate, leaving a recruited Alaskan whaler to deal with the meat and carcass. The Alaskan whaler was astounded at the lack of respect the Makah had for the whale and the hunt itself.

A traditional whale hunt is sacred. Not only was it a physical act while harvesting for food, it was a sacred act which evoked a spiritual experience in every hunter and the members of the hunter's family. Throughout the hunt which could last for three weeks or more, the wives of the hunters would lie down and remain still during the entire hunt so as to not disturb the concentration of their husbands, the village hunters. The Alaskan guest could not comprehend why the Makah men were not by his side, working with him to prepare the meat for their families. Today the meat probably remains in the bottom of a freezer, untouched and uneaten.

During the four years I worked in the whale-watching industry, I learned how to drive boats. My navigation skills were extended and I gained an understanding of not only weather forecasting, but the numerous moods of the ocean and how it influences the movements of a boat. My repertoire of skills and experiences opened many doors and lead to my work in the polar regions. It was through this work that I had the opportunity to be introduced to South Georgia.

Chapter 5

South Georgia

A land doomed to perpetual frigidness
whose savage reputation
I have not words to describe.
—Captain James Cook, 1775
On his first sailing journey
around South Georgia Island

South Georgia is an island of extremes – rugged mountains, sandy beaches sculptured by thundering surf, glacial valleys and snow fields that stretch for miles. Described in some literature as the Antarctic Serengeti, the island is teeming with seals, seabirds, penguins and albatross while the ocean is teeming with krill. Oddly though, the waters surrounding South Georgia remain devoid of whales, like a crater, a space where something was and is no longer. While the ocean once prospered with fin, sei, blue and humpback whales, today the only whales you see are the derelict parts that were of no use to the whaling industry.

Along the eastern shores lie hordes of bones, bleached by the sun and stacked like mountain summits, and the evidence of those that slaughtered the whales. The derelict ruins of whaling stations the size of towns lie abandoned as though the whalers left just yesterday. The slaughterhouse and flensing platforms sit centre stage, still intact and ready for use regardless of the rust and ruin. The lodgings for the blacksmiths, engineers and whalers border the vacant stations and at the outskirts are the graves of those who perished during these harsh and weathered times.

Whales were slaughtered to near extinction between the 1900s and 1960s. At times a yearly whale harvest was 14,219 and at other times, it soared to 40,201 individuals. Business was booming in an industry of bloody slaughter that employed over a thousand men. By 1965 the final whaling station at Leith Harbour was closed. By that time a total of 175,250 whales had been butchered and processed through South Georgia's whaling stations.

Seals were also targeted, particularly the elephant seal that can weigh up to 5000 kg. They were shot with rifles, the blubber was stripped from their bones and the oil was rendered down in try-pots which can still be found on the beaches of South Georgia today. Six thousand bulls were taken each year, yielding 2000 tons of top quality oil.

Although the negatives outweigh the positives in the whaling industry of South Georgia, the whaling stations played a significant role in the world of exploration, especially where the great Antarctic explorer, Sir Ernest Shackleton, was concerned.

In 1914 Shackleton's ship sat at anchor in the sheltered harbour of Grytviken, a whaling station situated in East Cumberland Bay, on the east coast of South Georgia Island. Ready to embark on the first ever attempt at crossing the continent of Antarctica. Twenty-seven men under Shackleton's command weighed anchor and said their farewells to the whalers, completely unaware that they would return, shipless and by foot two years later.

Shackleton's *Endurance* expedition turned into a desperate struggle for survival when his ship, only one hundred miles from its destination, became completely stuck in ice. In his journal, New Zealander Frank Worsley, the ship's navigator, described the ship's situation: "Like a nut stuck in toffee."

Eventually, the *Endurance* was crushed and it sank, forcing the men to abandon ship and move on to the sea ice and live under canvas as the floes drifted back out to open sea. Months later, when the sea ice in the distant horizon showed signs of breaking up, they decided to use their wooden lifeboats as sleds, pulling their minimal belongings out towards the open ocean.

Unsuccessful with this endeavour, the men were forced to wait for the ice to melt and the ocean to be navigable. When it did, Shackleton immediately allocated each man to one of three lifeboats and embarked on what still stands today as one of the most incredible small-boat journeys ever taken. Travelling on horrendous seas in a northerly direction, they reached the inhospitable and mountainous Elephant Island after seven days. They set foot on land for the first time in 497 days.

It was a savage place which offered no shelter or comfort. Elephant Island is situated where no ships go or even pass by, it is completely off the radar. Shackleton knew that a rescue would not come from outside help; they needed to organize it themselves. Shackleton selected five men to join him on a crossing from Elephant Island to South Georgia, an 800-nautical mile crossing, in the middle of winter, in a twenty-foot rowboat. The rest of his men were left on the shores of Elephant Island with the remaining two lifeboats as their only means of shelter, and penguins their main source of food.

Sailing across the worst seas in the world by rowboat, navigation done by sextant, with only one look at the sun, it is a miracle they made it to South Georgia. Having landed on the west side, devoid of whaling stations and other human life, the final stage of Shackleton's rescue mission was a walk across the island, traversing glaciers and climbing mountains, in an attempt to make it to the whaling station, Stromness. After three days and two nights, using minimal equipment – boots with nails in the sole instead of crampons – they stumbled into the whaling station, clothes in tatters and any exposed skin smothered in soot. It took a few minutes for the station manager to recognize Shackleton, but as soon as he did, he could not help but weep at the sight of the men that stood before him.

The retrieval of his men who were stranded on Elephant Island occurred four months later after three failed attempts due to various ships being stuck in ice, forcing them to retreat. Finally Shackleton, aboard the *Yelco*, approached the shore of Elephant Island. Gazing with painful intensity through his binoculars, Shackleton counted the men who appeared one by one from underneath the over-turned rowboats. He counted twenty two figures on shore. "All is well," he announced with relief.

"It sounds trite, but years literally seemed to drop from him as the men stood before us," Worsley, the chief navigator wrote in his journal.

Not one single man lost his life under Shackleton's lead. All survived and all returned home to war – World War I. The irony of this incredible survival story is that the men spoke very little of the expedition. Instead they held their head in shame because it was unsuccessful. They did not achieve what they set out to do. If only Shackleton knew, as he lies in his South Georgia grave, that his survival story is one of the greatest exploration stories that is still told today. The boat journey from Elephant Island to South Georgia still remains the most incredible small-boat journey ever made. It went down in history. Further still, he does not know that his leadership abilities are now used as a model in leadership conferences worldwide. We don't build men like Shackleton anymore; we are not built of the same stuff.

Shackleton's grave lies in a plot alongside the Norwegian whalers that occupied the Grytviken whaling station. He is visited by swarms of tourists who come to Antarctica and South Georgia with an interest in exploration history and natural history. These are the very ships that I work on. We depart from the port of Ushuaia in Argentina and upon arriving into King Edward Point[7], the capital of South Georgia, we are cleared by customs, receiving a stamp in each of our passports. Government officials come aboard our ship and if all paperwork is in order, such as the ship's inventory and passenger declaration forms, our ship, passengers and

---

[7] King Edward Point (also known as KEP) is a promontory and settlement with port facilities (wharf) on the northeastern coast of the island of South Georgia.

staff are cleared and allowed to continue with our adventures in South Georgia. All visits to South Georgia require the permission of the Commissioner.

The sovereignty of South Georgia has been disputed by Argentineans for many years. In April 1982, South Georgia became the southernmost region to experience war. A round of rockets was launched by the British, two Argentinean helicopters were shot down and numerous soldiers from both sides were killed. It was the British who surrendered. However, three weeks later, having sunk an Argentinean submarine, the British forces came back to take over South Georgia for good.

The war debris from military operations took years to clean up and unexploded ordinance can still be found on the island today.

South Georgia, now administered by the South Georgia government, is heavily involved with science and research. Their objectives include restoring native biodiversity, providing a safe and sustainable fishery, managing tourism to minimize environmental impact and basically doing top quality research. There is an extensive rat eradication program in their attempt at ridding the island of this invasive specie brought to the island by whalers. One of the native species under threat, not only due to the rats, is the wandering albatross.

Chapter 6

Storm Riders of the Southern Ocean – the Albatross

At length did cross an Albatross,
Through the fog it came;
As if it had been a Christian Soul,
We hailed it in his name.
—Samuel Taylor Coleridge
"Rime of the Ancient Mariner"

If you were to think of an animal which represented freedom of the purest kind, what animal would that be? I would choose the albatross. Endowed with a wandering spirit, they roam the skies uninhibited by the restraints of land and a perpetual longing for new horizons. They take the entire world and pave a life of adventure and travel that is without compare.

These storm riders of the Southern Ocean may orbit the earth up to three times in a single year. They spend ninety-five percent of their life at sea, having very little to do with land unless it is time to reproduce, which is an essential inconvenience. They return to their place of birth, often the most removed of islands thousands of miles away from continents because they offer the relentlessly windy conditions that the albatross require to fly. Their existence depends entirely on the probability that the winds will continue to blow.

Proportioned rather like a human with elongated arm bones, short hand bones and mediocre muscle strength, they are built to glide and drift through the air using gravity and the solar-powered wind. The wandering albatross – how suitable a name – has the largest wingspan of any bird, reaching up to twelve feet in length. Their wings are simply too cumbersome to flap; therefore, this remarkable bird floats more than it flies, expending energy while flying no greater than another bird at rest. Reaching speeds of up to 135 km per hour, an albatross will travel two thousand nautical miles on a single foraging flight. These gliding machines, if fortunate enough to live to the ripe age of fifty years, would have clocked over 3.7 million miles in a lifetime, all under sail.

In the animal kingdom, courting and sex often seem rather like a 'wham bam thank you ma'am' routine, but not with the albatross. A two year courtship leads to a lifetime together, although while raising a chick for an entire year, they may only spend ten days of that year together. Perhaps that is their secret for an everlasting, uncomplicated life together.

Their courting performance is a spectacle to watch. The dance style that comes closest is the tango. It is stern and sexy. Their movements are graceful yet abrupt, and their elegance evokes passion. Their twelve-foot wings are outstretched gracefully, the tail feathers are charmingly erect and their stylish heads are poised in the most seductive stance, as together they begin to dance. It is the essence of their romance.

After an eighty day incubation, a tiny, naked, vulnerable chick is hatched, now requiring both parents to take turns foraging for food and sitting on the nest. When the chick gets big enough, it needs a substantial supply of food, and as it is safe to leave the chick home alone, both parents go on foraging flights simultaneously. After being raised for an entire year, the chick, with awkward, lanky movements, steps away from its nest, waddles awkwardly through the tussock grass towards the steep cliff edges and faces the prevailing winds.

It unfolds its elaborate wings, flaps them in midair, warming and strengthening its newly formed flying muscles. With what looks like an uncoordinated gesture it takes a waddled running start towards the edge, flapping vigorously, only to stop mid-waddle just feet away from the drop. It is as though the bird has lost its nerve. After a few false starts and numerous demonstrations by its parents, the bird finally launches itself off the windblown cliff, drifting up towards the sky as though taking its first breath. Finally, the young albatross is flying and in the domain where it truly belongs. For this young albatross, the land is no longer of much use. The bird will spend its first five to seven years roaming the skies, never touching land until it reaches sexual maturity. This will be the only reason the bird comes ashore, returning to the very place it was born.

I was surprised when I looked up the definition for the word *albatross*; you too may be surprised. The first description is that of the bird we all now know so well. However, the second is the following: *"Something that hinders or handicaps, an encumbrance, wearisome burden."* This meaning was apparently derived from the poem, "The Rime of the Ancient Mariner" written in 1798 by Samuel Taylor Coleridge. Coleridge himself never actually set eyes on an albatross; however, "he sensed that here was a seabird with power enough to convey a universal cautionary tale. And we sense it still today."

Two centuries ago, the albatross symbolized a cherished companion for sailors at sea, a good luck charm keeping storms at bay. If a sailor were to harm an albatross, the worst luck would be afflicted upon the ship and its crew responsible for the bad deed done. In the poem, an albatross was shot down with a bow by one of the sailors. The dead albatross was hung around the sailor's neck for penance for the injustice he had done to nature. Shortly after, the ship was becalmed, sitting idle on the lifeless ocean, which only tests the patience and perseverance of a sailor. The stillness and silence, the monotonous days leading to tedious weeks drove the sailors to near insanity, until finally the curse was broken.

It is not easy to see an albatross. You either have to be on one of the far removed islands at the edge of continents or in the middle of a vast and open ocean in windy conditions. It is then you are blessed with its silent but serious company as the albatross glides alongside with outstretched wings, using the drafts of a ship during a long but effortless flight.

Dr. Frank Gill, President of the National Audubon Society, described his first encounter with an albatross: *"There was such wisdom in those beautiful eyes that have seen so many years. In all my life-time of experiences with birds, no moment was so moving."* Carl Safina, the President of the Blue Ocean Institute and renowned writer, has said: *"Following an Albatross will enlarge your life."*

My dream to kayak around South Georgia Island coincided with my passion for attempting such a mission. Without any doubt, my kayak expedition would be dedicated to the albatross and, I hoped, act as a catalyst to inform the public about the threats albatrosses are facing, to the point where they may be totally eliminated from our planet.

Chapter 7

Albatross in a Battle for Survival

Imagine sitting in a restaurant with a gathering of friends waiting hungrily for the delicious meal you ordered. You decided on the 'Dill and Lemon-Glazed Halibut, Baked.' You skipped lunch that day due to the drawn-out last minute meeting that used up your lunch hour. Your belly is gurgling with hunger. After thirty minutes the halibut arrives at the table and is placed in front of you. The fish is steaming along-side a generous portion of vegetables and roast potatoes. You start with the halibut. The knife cuts through the fish like a hot knife going through butter. It is cooked to perfection. You push the halibut on to your fork and eagerly pick up a mouth-ful. Due to your intense hunger, you don't bother to chew as much as you should and instead swallow the forkful whole. As the fish slips down, your stomach murmurs in delight.

Suddenly, you feel a sharp stabbing pain in the back of your throat as if you just swallowed a fish bone. What you don't realize is the weapon you just swallowed; the two-inch steel barred hook buried in your forkful of halibut has be-come lodged in your throat. You can no longer breathe, nor can you cough the hook up and out of your mouth. The di-rection of the barbs is only one way, down. You feel yourself literally choking, suffocating as though drowning, the oxygen no longer reaching your brain. Right there, in the middle of the restaurant, alongside your table of friends, you collapse to the floor and die.

Every five minutes an albatross experiences a similar death. Just take away the restaurant, your friends and replace them with the company of thousands of other birds experiencing the same death, in the enormity of the open sea.

Longline fishing is a technique which has been used since the 17th century. In modern times at least forty nations all around the globe take part in this business. Hundreds of millions of marine life are killed annually by an industry that is catching fish for our own dinner table.

Trailing off the stern of a longline fishing boat is a monofilament line that can be up to 100 km in length. The line carries at least fifteen thousand baited hooks. As the lines are set, the baited hooks linger on the surface of the water, creating easy pickings for those creatures that are on a constant lookout for food.

Like any animal living in the wild, they at times take foraging short cuts. It offers them an easy feed, but effortless foraging unfortunately is often deadly. A muster of thousands of innocent seabirds is attracted to these baited hooks and feeding frenzy. They open their broad beaks and take a mouthful of bait, swallowing without chewing, not realizing that it is attached to a hook. The hook snags them in the throat and drags them needlessly to the bottom and they drown. During surface longlining, the lines eventually descend to approximately three hundred metres and down to two thousand metres on a bottom longliner, finally out of the birds' reach.

What are the consequences behind the scenes of an albatross drowning? The dead albatross may be a newly fledged one-year-old or an albatross that has only recently reached sexual maturity. Perhaps it is a parent needing to return to the nest to feed its chick. Unfortunately if a parent does not make it back to the nest, the chick will starve to death. One parent alone cannot take care of the chick. A parent, sitting on an egg or perhaps a newly hatched chick, will wait patiently for its partner to return to the nest, because they are bonded for life. There is a record of an albatross parent sitting on an infertile egg for up to two months, losing a third of its body weight, waiting for its partner to return. It may take that individual up to four years to find a new mate, taking six to eight years out of its breeding cycle. All this is causing a rapid decline in the world's population of the albatross.

Approximately twenty-two species of albatross exist on our planet and all but one are listed as vulnerable, threatened, endangered or critically endangered. This does not include the numerous other seabird species that are also killed by the thousands daily. The northern fulmar, the prized petrel of the Canadian North, is one of the most common birds to get accidentally hooked. Unlike the albatross, these birds can dive and therefore they have double the chance of being hooked and drowned as they chase that baited hook to depths down to at least ten feet.

What else is being caught on longlines? In the Spanish longline fishing industry in the Mediterranean Sea, twenty thousand loggerhead turtles are captured every year. The nesting populations of the Pacific leatherback turtle have declined by ninety-five percent in the last two decades; their imminent extinction will occur in the next ten years. There is a rapid diminution of the world population of sharks. One hundred million sharks are caught on longlines to support the billion dollar fin industry. Yes, they are caught just for their fins; the rest of the body is unused and thrown back to sea. Shark-fin soup is a prized delicacy, but the cost?

Forty nations are longlining, setting 3.8 million hooks every day on a hundred thousand miles of longline. This occurs every day and every year 10 million hooks are being set in British Columbia, 12.5 million in Samoa, 25 million in Chile, 30 million in Argentina and 100 million in Japan. Longline fishing boats are fishing for cod, sablefish, halibut, Chilean sea bass, Patagonian toothfish, dolphinfish (mahi mahi), shark and tuna, just to name a few. They are fishing for us, for our friends and family. What fish do you choose to buy? Do you know how it is caught? Is it caught legally? Is it caught by a fishing industry that has implemented new techniques that reduce seabird and marine by-catch?

Recorded numbers of seabird mortalities, and of vessels longlining, do not include the illegal longline fishing industry that also features worldwide. In this business, they are unlikely to use any new methods to reduce seabird by-catch. The frustrating thing is, fish caught illegally are still being sold in the very markets and stores in which you and I shop.

Every day the world's human population expands to record size. The ultimate apex predator is humans. We have put pressure on nearly every ecosystem in the world to provide food and other resources and it is at the cost of species that have just as much right to inhabit our planet as we do.

An albatross has a life span of up to approximately sixty years. It lives long enough to have to contend with almost every consequence of human action relative to the sea. The loss of habitat due to industrial development, the human invasion on critical habitat for birds and other animals and the introduction of species such as mice and rats are all pressures that we place on the life of an albatross that already faces many other challenges. Oil spills are deadly for birds. They rely upon their waterproof feathers, oiled and preened to stay in flight and stay afloat. We have this obsession with plastic and other material items which are disposed of in a way that usually ends up in the sea. They choke, entangle and cause starvation in birds and other marine life. A photographer and bird biologist, Chris Jordan, has taken hundreds of photos of albatross carcass on Midway Island off the Hawaiian coast. Within the bellies of these albatross carcasses are items we recognize and use: plastic bottle caps, cigarette lighters, plastic stir sticks and rubber bands.

Approximately two hundred billion pounds (one hundred million tons) of plastic is produced each year in our world today. Most of the items we use for only a brief moment as when we open, say, the wrapping around our cell phone or swig down that bottled spring water. The wrapping, and the bottle, is then disposed of in the quickest and most effortless way possible, causing it eventually to end up in the sea. The vortex of plastic in our ocean is the size of a continent, spinning around our globe by the propulsion of our oceans' currents and trade winds, in the very substance that keeps our earth and earthlings alive. What can be done? How can you and I help?

While attending a presentation on the 'Polar Bears of Churchill and Global Warming,' the speaker, Robert Buchannan, addressed his audience with this answer to that very question. "Look in the mirror. You cannot always change the action of others, but you have full control in changing the action of yourself."

I believe he was right. Every one of us has the ability and control to make the changes that are required to leave a lesser imprint on our planet. At some stage while living our life, we have all done something which has compromised the health and wellbeing of another creature and our planet. We each have played a role in polluting our world, encroaching on another creature's habitat and causing grief and discomfort. With the ever-increasing spread of technology, industry and population, many of us have become far removed and disconnected from our natural world. Most people don't see that humans are just a part of nature, as are the birds, the beetles, the trees and the breeze. But we are. We are built of the same stuff. Take water for example. Eighty-five percent of our brain, eighty percent of our body and seventy percent of our muscle is all made up of water.

Every living thing has its proper place in the world and all life is sacred. We recognize the value in ourselves and each other, and we take care of our needs and desires. Perhaps we could direct the same attention and care towards our organic neighbors.

My first significant solo sea kayak journey was around Vancouver Island. It was during this two month period that I recognized the value of living simply and having few re-sources, yet at the same time feeling completely comfortable, safe and happy.

Chapter 8

Kayaking Alone – A Maiden Voyage

You ask me "Why Alone?"
Imagine fluid pathways of salt and sand taking you to a
place of solitude where the wind is the only voice you
hear and the waves your only song.

The eerie silence of fog engulfed every rock and reef and erased all points of land that were to be my destination. Within seconds, I was left with only my hearing, my compass and dead reckoning as my only tools to navigate around this extremely exposed, rugged coastline. A bulb from bull kelp[8] kept me stationary as a two-metre swell pulsed beneath my hull, crashing violently on the nearby shore.

Three choices in regards to what I should do went through my head. One, stay clinging securely to this ocean anchor and wait for the sun to burn away the fog; at least here I know exactly where I am. Two, head towards what looks like a sandy beach but could be a treacherous rock garden. Or, three, continue in a south-easterly direction, keeping well off shore to clear the chaotic area of unpredictable breaking water around erratic boulders.

---

[8]Bull Kelp is one of the largest brown algae's. It grows attached to the sea floor by a specialized root-like structure called a holdfast. From the holdfast is a long stem-like stipe which is hollow and filled with gases which extends to the surface of the sea, terminating at an enlarged, spherical hollow float. It occurs in the upper subtidal zone to a depth of 100 feet and is common along the coast of the northeastern Pacific Ocean.

Only the night before had I made an entry in my journal expressing the need for a challenge and wishing to be put to my long-anticipated 'test.'

On June 19th I left Victoria Harbour to begin a solo sea kayak journey exploring the complete coastline of Vancouver Island. After three summers of sea kayak guiding and crewing on charter boats in various areas throughout the island, I decided it was time to fill in all the gaps and piece the entire island together. I wanted to be totally absorbed within the ocean environment and to develop an understanding of all its characteristics. I needed to go solo in order to achieve this goal, allowing nature to be my only companion, only distraction. I realized the challenges that tagged along with this dream but I felt experienced enough and ready. I set off equipped for a two month expedition; my PFD (personal flotation device) bulged with a handheld radio, a GPS receiver, an EPIRB[9], a compass, rocket flares and half a dozen energy bars, making me feel like gadget girl. My nineteen-foot kayak was packed with enough gear and food to carry me past the island's more populated coastline, the Strait of Georgia. After months of training and preparation I soon found myself bidding farewell to friends and family who had gathered to see me off. I watched the familiar figures get smaller and smaller as I anxiously paddled away.

The morning of the fog incident had started with clear and calm conditions. The full moon sat high in the sky and at 6:00 am the sun lay low on the horizon. The forecast sounded promising and the glassy ocean was a welcoming watery path. This northern portion of the west coast of British Columbia, ten miles south of Kyuquot Sound, juts out into the Pacific, causing confused currents, strong wind and unpredictable water as the wind and water move with considerable speed around natural contours of the land. It was the month of August (sometimes referred to as Fogust), so I wasn't surprised to see fog packed thickly towards the south. The area along the west coast of Vancouver Island has a shelf

---

[9]Emergency Position Indicating Radio Beacon.

lying beneath the ocean floor causing the swell to suddenly peak and break half a mile offshore, then break again on and over the battered reefs that lace the majority of the coastline. I was about to increase my understanding and respect for the power of fog.

I recalled the many days I had travelled as a passenger by motorboat in thick fog, enjoying the silence and mystery of this blinding ocean blanket. The air around me felt damp and had a salty scent that made my exposed skin tingle. I love the sound of foghorns echoing from lighthouse stations, providing a safe passage for sailors who are being led by this continuous chorus and are brightly lit up like street lamps in the darkest of nights. This time was different, I was the captain of my own boat and it was up to me to find my way to safety. I had discovered by my journey this far that I wasn't good at waiting, whether waiting on shore for winds to die or sitting in a Kevlar kayak holding onto a piece of bull kelp. Within minutes I had grown impatient with the waiting and released this forested anchor, continuing blindly in search of a rock-free, surf-friendly beach to land on and wait for the fog to clear. If it weren't for the erratic boulders scattered along the particular coastline, that caused spontaneous explosions of waves, I'd have been quite happy to continue on my way following a compass bearing.

I pointed my boat in a southerly direction and went out and around the breaking waves I could only hear. The wind had already started to pick up, like it often does by late morning. When I saw a glimpse of the swell, I estimated it to be at a height of about two meters but in fog it seemed to look and feel much larger, towering above me like city skyscrapers. I decided to head into what looked like a beach from my estimated position on the chart. The idea of being out here in big winds and swell I could only feel and not see, encouraged my desire to land. I tried to get an accurate position using my GPS but it was taking a long time to pick up a signal. I edged very slowly, my bow directed towards the shore. I soon noticed the waves were peaking and crashing in front of me. I made the assumption that I was getting closer to shore.

For one split second the fog cleared enough for me to get a glance at the beach I was about to land on. There was a beach alright but the entire edge was lined with rocks, rugged enough to pierce any bullet-proof boat. Simultaneously a two-metre wave was about to pick me up and lunge me forward towards the land I no longer desired. Without any time to prepare, I leaned back in a surf position, placed my paddle in the water using it as a brake and unintentionally closed my eyes. By this time I figured the wave was now in control of my destiny and my reactions were too late.

Somehow the position of my paddle must have offered some resistance against the wave as I found myself in the trough of the wave which now exploded violently in front of me. I urgently paddled backwards to reinforce my secure position. My heart nearly bounced out of my chest. Relieved, I continued with my back to the exploding shoreline, noticing that my mounted camera had taken the brunt of the wave. It had become unhinged and was now hanging over the side of my bow. I paddled for twenty minutes as the fog gradually lifted and soon found a perfectly sheltered bay with only one metre of swell breaking on shore. The beach was pebbled and, once safely ashore, I knelt down to the sand and kissed the ground I stood upon. A hot chocolate was soon in my hand as the fog moved in once again, encasing me within this sheltered bay. In many ways, now that I was onshore, the enclosing sensation of fog gave me a feeling of protection, keeping the chaos of reefs and waves at bay, obstructing me from their dangers.

The fog incident became one of the many challenges I experienced as I continued to paddle further down the west coast of Vancouver Island. Frequent obstacles teased and tested me as the ocean and wind played their game of tag. Southeasterly winds confused the seas and presented me with tortuous paths to navigate and the prevailing northwesterly winds exposed my back to the sun and wind. The typically increasing wind often forced me back to shore.

The fog continued to play a significant role in my journey, leaving parts of the coast a mystery. Each day I rose to the occasion and problem-solved like any good mariner and, along the way, I collected memories of special moments and accumulated treasures that can only be found along this coast. One of those treasures was my frequent encounters with grey whales that cruised tightly along the shore; I paddled as they foraged amongst the cluttered kelp beds. There was a time when I was heading in to land and was unable to because three grey whales unintentionally blocked my way. I was forced to watch and wait as they bulldozed the ocean floor, taking mouthfuls of krill and other zoo plankton, then rising to the surface to take a breath. I waited for seven minutes before an opening was available. At the time, I was busting to pee and was grateful for the gap which enabled me to head to shore. I was an uninvited guest in their ocean realm, their only intruder, but one who was thankful for being alone to soak up every blow and breath released by these gentle giants.

By the time I pulled into Victoria Harbour sixty-two days later, my memory bank was full to the brim, my ocean-going skills were fine-tuned and my body was strong. For two months I glided effortlessly on the salted skin of the ocean, my eyes and ears adjusting to the rhythms of the land interacting with the sea. I had become in tune with the movements of the wildlife and the changing weather and I felt the heartbeat of the glorious web of life that naturally keeps everything in order. I felt content with the simple items I carried and the company I kept. They fulfilled my every need, offering comfort, shelter, food and entertainment. It is all I required. Throughout the two months I spent alone I was never lonely. I felt like a student in an aquatic classroom with numerous teachers and I passed the term with flying colors.

Even before I approached the dock in Victoria's Inner Harbour where loyal friends waited for me, I had already set my sight on my next expedition. Another island beckoned me. One that also stands alone in the middle of an immense open sea containing sacred treasures seen by only those who dare make the effort to visit those distant shores.

Chapter 9

Kayaking Alone – A Sacred Passage

I was to experience the fulfillment of enforced self-reliance, learning and adapting to the ways of the sea as it interacts with the land. And in doing so I would learn to know myself as I truly was.

On the wild and unpredictable coast of Graham Island[10] I was experiencing the scariest and most challenging paddling I had ever done. For the first time in my sea kayaking experience I felt convinced that if I accidentally capsized, I would be unable to get myself out of a potentially life threatening situation. Every headland I was aiming for seemed to take hours and immense effort to reach. I tried to paddle with more force and quicken my speed but the motions of the sea were confused and sporadic, my boat was heavy, laden with gear and my wrists tender. It was a sluggish ride. Without a doubt, I was also taking on water through what was supposed to be 'water tight' hatches. I felt like a tortoise trudging along slowly and this frustrated me. I wanted to be the rabbit not the tortoise.

I cursed out loud at the slowness of my boat and the pain in my swollen wrists, swearing at the wind and the seas that intimidated me. I desperately wanted to be around the exposed Kindakin Point but the sea was holding me back. For the first time in my relationship with the sea, I disliked it. Thick, grey,

---

[10]Graham Island is part of Haida Gwaii in British Columbia, just north of Vancouver Island.

soot-like clouds hovered over me as though they were trying to suffocate. Two- to three-metre seas rose and fell beneath me and the wind continued to rough up my ride. The morning's forecast spoke of two-metre seas and wind coming from the northwest at a rate of 10 to 20 knots. This looked and felt much worse.

It took over an hour to finally reach Kindakin Point, a finger of rugged land that juts out into the sea like a broad paw of a lion. As I rounded, a familiar scent wafted toward me, one I never would have expected to smell out here – cigarette smoke! 'Thank goodness,' I thought, 'fishermen, people, company.' I could just make out two or three small boats in the distance, appearing then disappearing as the swell rose and fell. It was as though the ocean was breathing, a liquid chest rising then falling. I altered my course and paddled eagerly towards the closest boat. As I approached I noticed three men were gazing in my direction and then they turned to each other. Perhaps they were questioning why a paddler would be out here. As I paddled nearer, I attempted to speak and indulge in social conversation such as "Hi guys, had any luck catching fish?" I had not spoken to anyone for over two weeks. From their facial expressions I assumed that what just came out of my mouth did not make any sense. It was probably more like a jabbering noise rather than words that anyone could comprehend. One of the men, I assumed it was the guide, told me of a very recent revised forecast he had just heard on his VHF radio. It spoke of seas building to four metres and winds expected to rise to gale force by noon that day. I glanced down at my watch which was attached to my lifejacket. It was 10:45 am. I looked at my chart and calculated the distance to the beach I was hoping to camp on. All I had to do was continue around the headland and enter into the inlet that led to Carew Bay, where a beach lay waiting. Turning back was not an option; the wind would be against me and the distance further.

This brief human encounter turned out to be valuable. I bade them farewell, thanked them for the information and called out half in jest, "Keep an eye on me would you," as I anxiously paddled away.

Minutes after, it was as though the weather knew I had just heard its potential plans and wanted to show me it meant business. Clouds black as night congregated above me, heavy and burdened with water bursting to spill out. This dark shadow loitered over me like unwelcome shade on a summer's day. By now the ocean was the same color as the sky, dim and gloomy like the color of slate. The entire scene felt as though it was frowning over me, presenting me with its meanest look. Every third paddle stroke was a support stroke as I braced every time an unstable wave hit me broad side. Reef after reef I passed, each one sending waves thrashing back towards me and bucking beneath my hull. The seas were literally building right before my eyes. Mountaintops two thousand metres high disappeared as the peaks from the rising swell climbed higher and higher towards the sky.

'How long do I need to keep this up?' I wondered. The weather and the sea were getting worse and I still had a long way to go. I noticed an awful taste in my mouth, bitter and acidic as though my natural juices had turned rancid; perhaps this is what fear tastes like. I glanced behind at the fishing boats and saw them struggling in the building seas. One by one they slowly motored away, down the inlet to safety; they too had had enough and were leaving this treacherous place. I was alone once again. I shouted into the wind, apologizing to my family for putting them through the loss of me to the depths of the heartless sea. This gesture itself seemingly gave me the incentive to push on. There was no other choice but to paddle hard.

As I paddled I went through the scenario 'what would I do if I capsized?' Of course, I would immediately attempt a roll. Before this trip I had practiced rolling with my kayak loaded, but not in conditions quite this awesome. What if I fell out of my cockpit and rolling was no longer an option? I would have to get back in my boat. Could I do that in seas as confused as these? My boat would be swamped without a doubt, and if I can't get back in, could I swim to shore and scramble up on the rocks? I didn't think so, not with huge, curling, cresting waves crashing over the jagged reefs. I explored the various outcomes of my nightmare and eventually came up with the best plan – DO NOT CAPSIZE!

The Queen Charlotte Islands, also referred to as Haida Gwaii, are often described with words such as Sacred, Spiritual, Powerful, Special and Challenging. They are a geographical treasure with haunting scenic vistas and challenging outdoor pursuits. *"A thriving coastal culture, Haida Gwaii offers the promise of a magical journey to the center of your soul"* is the description in the local travel guide. Every piece of literature you read prepares you for an unforgettable experience where your personal comfort levels, and skills, both physical and emotional and perhaps even spiritual, will be pushed and challenged like never before. In fact some texts deter one from even going, as they warn you of the dangers when you venture into this unique, dramatic and unpredictable region. My solo journey by kayak around Haida Gwaii was all that and much more.

This triangular archipelago is made up of more than one hundred and fifty islands, most of them uninhabited. Glaciers and volcanic activity have shaped the landscape over the past two million years. Snowcapped mountains, valleys, fjords that plunge into the sea, riverbeds and shorelines are the remaining evidence of Mother Nature's actions. The waters surrounding Haida Gwaii are known for their drastic and dramatic interaction with the notorious bad weather that frequents the region and can change without warning.

The total area of Haida Gwaii is approximately 3,840 square miles, and it is 156 miles (250 km) in length from north to south. In the east is Hecate Strait, a shallow marine valley of open water that in some literature has been classified as the fourth worst body of water to cross in the world. On the west coast is the open Pacific Ocean with a continental shelf less than 5 km offshore that plummets two thousand metres down into the immense depths of the Pacific Ocean.

Graham Island is one of the two main islands that make up Haida Gwaii; the second is South Moresby. Gwaii Haanas, a

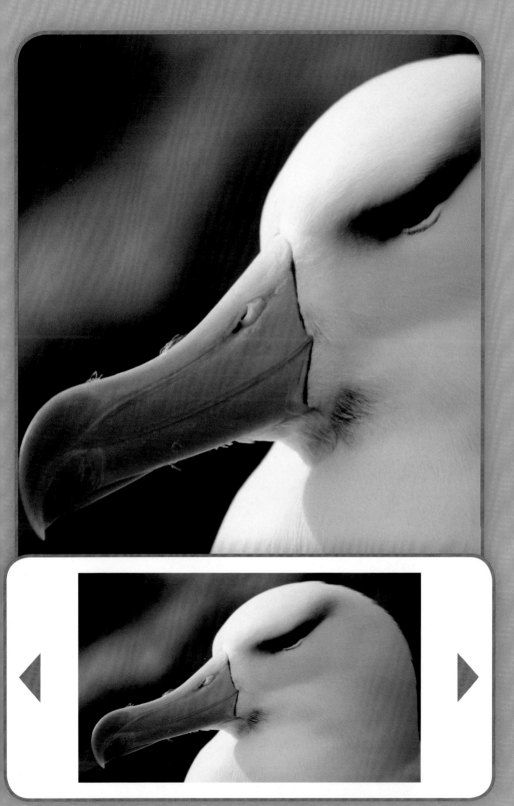

► a portrait of a blackbrowed albatross

► our aquatic escort - photo by Beth-Anne Masselink.

► Peales Dolphin near the Falkland Islands - photo by Beth-Anne Masselink.

▶ the abandoned whaling station of Grytviken

▶ the Petrel - an old whaling ship

▶ a paddling portrait

▶ fur seals are my constant companion

▶ a visit with some fur seals

► curious elephant seal - photo by Brandon Harvey

▶ it's a tough life for a juvenile elephant seal

▶ first camp - Leith Harbour

National Park Reserve and Haida Heritage Site is considered to be one of the most precious places on our planet, a place of value to the entire world that covers the majority of South Moresby Island. It has no roads, few facilities and is teeming with wild life. An estimated one and a half million seabirds nest along the shoreline from May to August. The ocean is alive with fish, molluscs, migrating whales and numerous other species. Mist enshrouded forests contain ancient trees that can reach up to ninety five metres in height; some are as old as a thousand years. At the base of these giants are rich and luscious thickets of bright green mosses, ferns and berry bushes. If you look closely enough, you can see the remains of old longhouse pits and fallen totem poles camouflaged by the natural layers of forest growth.

It takes a fair effort to get to Haida Gwaii. Folk who venture here are those drawn to its remoteness and are interested in the history, particularly along the east coast of South Moresby where many abandoned village sites remain. One in particular, SGang Gwaay (Ninstints) on Anthony Island in the south, has original totem poles. They stand erect, facing out to the picturesque scene of scattered islands which lead to the open sea, their stature expressing power and wisdom. It is like no other place on the planet and when you are fortunate and willing to travel the distance to Haida Gwaii and stand amongst these totems, you feel through your skin and in your bones the sacredness of the place.

Exhausted after having paddled hard for five hours, I landed, utterly drenched from the many waves that broke over my bow and smacked me like a crashing wall of water. Once ashore, the clouds released their pressure, and like a burst pipe, the rain came down. Upon opening my hatches I discovered both were full of water, the back hatch dangerously so. Both my wrists were puffed up and looked as though I had a plum tucked beneath the skin and their stiffness made the task of opening dry bags difficult. I felt shattered and sore, but perfectly safe.

After nineteen days paddling around Graham Island, a damaged boat and injured wrists forced me to me abandon my goal of kayaking around the two main islands of Haida Gwaii in one summer. Instead, it was broken up into two trips and two summers. Graham Island was completed in the summer of 2004, and in 2005, I circumnavigated South Moresby in twenty-five days. There was an added challenge to the latter journey; three weeks prior to my departure I had separated from my partner of seven and a half years.

Although these trips were relatively short compared to my previous sixty-two day journey around Vancouver Island, they challenged me further, mentally, emotionally and physically, leaving me with vital lessons and experiences one rarely has the chance to encounter in everyday life. John Muir sums it up rather well:

> *A journey is a person in itself, no two are alike, and all plans, safeguards, policies and coercions are fruitless. We find after years of struggle, we don't take a journey, a journey takes us.*

I couldn't help but compare each journey. While circumnavigating solo around Vancouver Island, everything seemed to go as planned. That led me to believe that the same would be experienced in Haida Gwaii. How wrong I was. My equipment failed and my body did not stand up to the constant battering. I expected tougher conditions but the weather during the month of August while paddling around Graham Island happened to be one of the worst on record. I had fewer encounters with people, the village watch-keepers had gone and I never saw a single whale. My main focus ended up being to simply travel these waters safely and come to terms with the fact that things don't always go as planned. What I considered to be a failed attempt at achieving both islands in one summer, definitely reminded me that I too have an ego, as I was terribly disappointed.

I came to accept that this journey was ultimately about experiencing fear, uncertainty and setbacks, and discovering how I respond to them. During the journey around South Moresby, due to my recent relationship separation, I was sensitive and vulnerable. This emotional state altered my response to the struggle and fear that naturally occurs when partaking in expeditions. I recognized the benefits also. I was forced to dig deeper like I had never done before and search for the courage within myself to overcome the fears I faced daily. I did this in a raw state, stripped down to my very core, confronting the challenges naked and exposed. For the first time I saw myself as I truly was.

I gained more respect for the power of the sea, recognizing its strength and realizing that the ocean takes and destroys without sympathy or apology. At the same time, the sea is not out to deliberately harm us, hurt us or cause suffering. Yet at times we blame it for our losses. When we place ourselves on the sea in a variety of constructed vessels, it does what it does and we are simply there, responding to it. I was grounded by the sea. The romantic relationship I once thought I shared with the sea has simmered to a more realistic one, consisting of all the ups and downs and uncertainties that exist in any relationship. The sea scared me but I faced it; we had serious confrontations, but we always made up. H.W. Tilman once said, *"The seas most powerful spell is romance."*

My journey around Haida Gwaii once again enforced the values I hold in living a simple life, using few resources and causing less impact on the planet. We can all travel lightly on this earth and still remain well fed, comfortable, sheltered and even be entertained, simply by being immersed in the divine delight of nature and the wild. During this intimate time with nature, once again I paddled to the beat of her drum, bathed within her waters and basked beneath her sun. My every move was dictated by Mother Nature's hand. I was exposed to her need for balance with all the dynamics of land and sea and once again I was inspired to do more for our precious coast and planet.

Chapter 10

Kayaking to Save the Albatross

Whatever you do, or dream you can, begin it.
Boldness has genius and power and magic in it.
—Goethe

In May 2006, while biking home one evening after dinner with friends, my mind turned to South Georgia. I had visited the island many times since that first experience six years ago, and each time I was plagued by a desire to kayak around it and haunted by the fear of what that task would actually entail. That night, something changed inside of me and I could no longer resist the temptation.

I was influenced by a few factors. At the time I was attending a goal setting seminar and South Georgia was in my brainstorm of goals I hoped to achieve in the next five years. I was also single, which meant no obligations, no commitments and no compromises. I had the freedom to do exactly what I desired with my life.

I walked into my apartment, placed my bike along the hallway wall and went straight to my computer. I clicked onto Google and searched for *Northanger*. This was the vessel that supported the three New Zealanders who were the first to kayak around South Georgia in 2005. At the top of the homepage I read the quote *"Whatever you do, or dream you can, begin it. Boldness has genius and power and magic in it."* That struck a chord within and inspired me like no other quote ever had. At that precise moment, I knew there was no turning back.

Five months later, I bought half a house. My friend Maureen in Alert Bay[11] had found a cottage suitable for her holiday accommodation business during the summer months and perfect for me to live in for the rest of the year. For the first time since living in Canada, I had a home base which wasn't a van or a boat or a friend's couch. I had a home and an office where the South Georgia expedition plans would be created.

I soon realized that

- All expeditions require a permit from the Commissioner for South Georgia.
- All expedition permit applications are subject to an assessment process by a panel of consultants who have extensive experience of planning and leading expeditions to South Georgia. The process will draw advice from this panel of expert advisors, for which an administrative fee of 1000 pounds is charged. If the information provided in an expedition application is inaccurate or misleading, the Commissioner reserves the right to revoke an expedition permit and or restrict the future access of individual applicants.
- All expeditions must be supported throughout by an adequately insured expedition support vessel.
- Authorized by GSGSSI – Government of South Georgia and South Sandwich Islands

Never before have I had to 'ask for permission' to follow a dream or to take part in a kayak expedition, even from my own mother! Yet in early 2008 I found myself filling out a rather detailed application form, in order to prove to a panel of British government officials that I was capable, intelligent and more than adequately skilled to attempt the first ever solo sea kayak journey around South Georgia Island.

---

[11]Alert Bay, in the northern regions of Vancouver Island

I was dreadfully nervous that I would be turned down and told that I was not allowed to go. I was going alone therefore the risks were greater. Is that not the first rule when adventuring outdoors – '**Never go alone!**' Imagine being told – "You are NOT allowed to attempt your expedition, you are NOT allowed to fulfill your ten-year dream." Having the expedition's destiny and my dream controlled by someone else, made my stomach churn. It was disconcerting beyond any uncertainty I had ever felt.

To my delight and great relief, I was granted permission. Little did I know that this application process was only the beginning of what would become an expedition (and a dream) that would end up in the hands of many.

I was required by the British government to have a boat that would act as a support vessel. The entire expedition had to be completely self-sufficient and we were not to rely upon any outside assistance, particularly the government officials and scientists that are situated at the King Edward Point base on the eastern side of South Georgia Island. I use the term 'support vessel' very lightly. It was highly impractical and unlikely that the boat and crew onboard would be able to assist me in any emergency situation. The reality of the circumstance was that my support vessel would at times be days away from where I would be positioned. The entire coast of South Georgia offers only a handful of safe anchorages where sailboats can be tucked away from the frequent windstorms. You will not find a sailboat any place else.

For me, my personal options are greater. I have a vessel that can be dragged ashore, even on a boulder beach at a pinch. Ultimately my support vessel was my means to get to South Georgia, a way to receive the most recent technical weather forecasts, and they would be there to recover my body if I was found either dead or alive. Essentially, they would be my 'search and rescue' vessel. And so, to even begin the process of turning my dream into a reality, the first thing I needed to do was charter a boat and crew.

The price for chartering a boat and crew to sail in Antarctic waters is approximately $150,000. Perhaps this is one of the reasons why South Georgia's coast remains somewhat unexplored and the mountain peaks unclaimed by most adventurers. It is just too damn expensive. I sure don't have that kind of cash kicking around.

This financial obstacle was what haunted my dreams, my commitment. I was grateful when a husband and wife team, Greg Landreth and Keri Pashuk, who own the sailing vessel *Northanger,* came onboard. They offered to be my support boat at 'mates' rates,' an amount that made my goal more accessible. Sure, I could purchase my own boat for the price I had to pay. But it wouldn't be suitable for southern ocean travel, and would certainly not get me to South Georgia.

Sitting at a computer, writing up proposals, applying for grants and simply fundraising was to be my life for four years. And this was during the global economic collapse. I had extremely bad timing for my first attempt at fundraising for an expedition.

I was never very good at door-to-door sales; I find it difficult approaching anyone to buy or invest in something I own or have created. I made no money selling Girl Guide cookies, I gave away items at garage sales and, during job interviews, I would always forget to ask how much I was going to be paid. I have never really been a moneymaker and I lack the drive to make even a handful of it. I work because it gives me joy; money is a secondary bonus. I need very little and feel completely content with what I already have. Although I believed wholeheartedly in the expedition and was driven to the cause of raising awareness for the albatross, I still did not feel comfortable asking for money, gear and assistance.

I required highly specialized equipment, able to withstand not only the frigid environment but the windy conditions as well. And I mean really windy. Imagine eighty-knot winds blasting down glaciated valleys, sending anything in its path racing out to sea. In 2001, an American extreme ski TV team was beaten back down by appalling weather conditions from a mountain they were attempting to climb, only to find that all of their tents and belongings back at camp had blown out to sea. South Georgia is not the place to be homeless.

A super strong tent, an extremely warm sleeping bag (with a rating of thirty degrees below Celsius), a kayak built to sustain collisions with rocks and ice (well! hopefully not many collisions), nutritious food with high fat content, warm, breathable, rugged and comfortable clothes and paddling attire were required. Usually these rugged items are the most expensive on the market. I spent days, weeks leading to months on the computer simply sending emails and proposals asking for a single item to be donated.

What followed were countless rejections unless I was ignored completely. "How could you not want to support a unique expedition for a really important cause?" I often asked. But they must receive zillions of these requests, and I was just one of the many who simply needed free stuff.

I had a few successes for which I am extremely grateful. One in particular came from a private donor, a couple I had met while working on a ship in the Arctic. This donation would go a long way to make my dream come true.

For six months I waited for 'the check' which they had assured me would come. A month prior to my departure, in January 2009, I was forced to postpone the expedition until the following year. The promised funds had not arrived. I was so disillusioned, perhaps even depressed. Not only did I have an entire year ahead with South Georgia looming on the horizon once again, occupying my dreams and taking up most of my days, but it was the other people involved whom I felt I had let down.

My support vessel, the *Northanger*, was left without a contract for the season; my two support guys, Zachery Shaw and Paul Chaplow, both from New Zealand, had put their lives on hold and bought non-refundable plane tickets to join me. Suddenly they had to reinvent two months of their life and suck up the loss of their plane tickets. Although I was fighting off anxiety, uncertainty and doubt, and I felt burdened to maintain my motivation and keep the momentum alive, the delay turned into a blessing.

By the time I departed I was better prepared. My body was healthier and stronger. I had all the equipment and devices I needed and I knew how most of them worked. By this time a film producer had shown an interest and helped me to purchase the right camera equipment. More people had been made aware of my expedition and its purpose due to my having done numerous presentations and really getting my blog well established. And, finally I had the money. Even after having another year to raise funds, I was far from successful. Expedition grants were mainly being distributed amongst climbing teams who had mountains to conquer and first ascents to achieve. So, I finally secured a loan from the bank. This time nothing was going to stop me.

In Alert Bay, almost every house has an ocean view. If you want to know the weather forecast, simply look out of your window. The north coast of Vancouver offers many winter days when the sky is burdened with clouds hovering low along the horizon. The seas are troubled with whitecaps and wind swell, often sending the ocean into confusion. If you want to know the temperature of the day, you step outside. The dampness and the wind penetrate through your winter layers and your cheeks and nose immediately go numb. It is these very conditions that made me say quite frequently, "Ah it is another good day for a paddle." These conditions are ideal when one is training for a kayak trip in the sub-Antarctic, but of course one has to be really motivated.

To prepare for the South Georgia expedition I needed to be disciplined. I was never too good with routines but for this particular endeavour, I had incentive. The desire to stay alive and return to my loved ones and play out the rest of my life was a significant driving force. I was determined to beat the polar elements and stay as warm as possible. For too many years, I had guided in Antarctica with continually frozen feet and hands. Without a doubt I was preparing to paddle in the most difficult region and on the most challenging seas on the planet.

In a typical day I did yoga in the early morning, spent most of the day on the computer and/or the phone. Before dinner I ventured out into the winter weather and paddled for two hours. In the late evening I would spend an hour in the gym, mainly on the row machine and, at times, that would be replaced with a run in the nearby wooded trails.

Most of the gear I required was ordered over the Internet. Therefore, trips to the post office were exciting events. What parcel of goodies would I be receiving next? I under-estimated the effort and time required to learn how to use my new gadgets. It took me days to understand the workings of my new mini-computer which had a different operating system than my laptop. I spent hours inputting all the landing and camping sites, headlands and other significant co-ordinates in my GPS. And, having never held a video camera before, its mastery was also a time-consuming task. And how on earth did this pee-funnel cup thingy work?

The dream to film the adventure in the hope of making a documentary of the expedition became a reality when I chanced upon a film producer. Her name is Katie Mustard. We met on a rafting trip down the Grand Canyon. I was invited as a guest by the Annenberg Foundation to join a group of four American Indians, an expert naturalist of the region, and a big wave rider from Hawaii on a rafting trip down the Grand Canyon. Katie was producing the documentary film being made on this rafting journey. As we hiked the dry dusty trails alongside the immense river and drifted downstream between each rapid, I spoke of my wish to kayak around South Georgia for the 'Plight of the Albatross.' Katie was curious and asked many questions. Three months later, I was picking her up at the Port Hardy airport. She had a professional camera in tow, and was my visitor for the next ten days. Together we would see the New Year through and Katie would become my official producer. The documentary idea 'Soul of the Sea' had been crafted.

It was a hectic time leading up to departure. I kept my blog alive, keeping people informed with daily blog entries. I contacted various media and appeared on the local T.V. and radio channels. With the aim of involving the community of Alert Bay, I did presentations at the two elementary schools. From then on every kid I passed in the street or met at the grocery store approached me and asked: "Are you the Albatross lady?" I practiced Eskimo rolls[12] near the township and a curious audience often gathered. Alert Bay in the middle of winter was a more than suitable training ground.

The final task before setting off was to pacify my mother. How does one tell one's mum the whole truth, and nothing but the truth, when about to set off on a potentially dangerous expedition? "Yes mum, the support vessel will be shadowing me the entire way. They will be anchored in the very bay where I will camp. If I get cold I can go onboard the sailboat to warm up and have a cup of tea." Not likely.

To minimize her concern for my safety, I did not correct these myths. I kept the facts vague.

Back in 2004, upon returning with injured wrists and a leaking kayak after my Haida Gwaii circumnavigation, I received a stroppy email from my mum who lives in New Zealand. It was during a time in her life when she was trying to be more assertive and to speak her mind. "Isn't it time you settled down!" she wrote. "Find a hobby a little closer to home and an activity that is not so dangerous. I am not ready to lose a daughter!" She was assertive that day.

I am grateful for my parents. They have always supported my choice in life-style even though my work and interests take me around the globe and often to remote regions. I am fortunate that they recognize that I am living my life to the fullest and while doing so I am following my dreams. How can a parent even begin to challenge that? I recognize also that my mum's reaction in her email was also just. She is a mum after all and it is a mother's privilege and a mother's way – to be concerned and to worry. I realize the selfishness when one follows their dreams, especially when it places them in risky situations. However, to not live your life to the fullest would be to only half live – and is that not an even greater risk?

---

[12]Every kayaker should learn how to flip their kayaks back over if they end up upside down, otherwise known as the **Eskimo Roll**.

Chapter 11

Dean – My True Support Vessel

Behind every successful man is a woman.

Is that not how the quote goes? Well in my case, behind every successful expedition is a group of people supporting me, helping me and basically making the expedition happen. Dean was one of those people.

I met Dean Laar in February 2008, through two mutual friends in the whale-research industry. Janie Wray and Hermann Meuter established a whale research station in the Great Bear Rain forest in B.C.[13] The research facility is located on Gill Island, the very same island the BC ferry *Queen of the North* hit in 2006. Dean spent months living on Gill, helping with labour around the place, milling and chopping wood, building structures and clearing trails.

Janie and I met at OrcaLab on Hanson Island in 1995 and we connected immediately. It was as though we had known each other all of our lives. We could talk about anything and share with each other our deepest and most profound thoughts. During Dean's months living on Gill, Janie had spoken about me numerous times, innocently bragging about my kayak exploits around exposed islands and my love for nature and wildlife. At the beginning of 2008, Dean turned up in

---

[13]British Columbia

Alert Bay on a spontaneous trip, tagging along with another mutual friend. It was 'like' at first sight.

Dean walked through the door of my cottage along with my friend Lisa whom I hadn't seen in ten years. He stood at approximately my height, wearing a 'Life is Good' baseball cap with wisps of salt and pepper hair framing each of his ears. With eyes the colour of chocolate and a soccer player's build I found him attractive. Neither Dean nor I was in search of a partner. However, several camp fires, dinners, profound and fiery discussions and music jam sessions later, I recognized that here was a soul who also appreciated the simplicities of nature and lived his life as true to himself as one can be. We travelled the island together on a mini road trip getting to know each other. Although he wasn't an outdoorsman in a sense of the climber, the kayaker or the surfer, he relished the simplicity of cooking on an open fire, listening for owls at night and fishing beside a running brook. A moonlit stroll, hand in hand along a beach in Ucluelet was one of the many things that turned the innocent fooling around into something much deeper. He entered my life and by default got stuck with the South Georgia expedition.

Having travelled within Canada, working an assortment of jobs, Dean had gathered a vast collection of skills. He can put his hand to pretty much anything. His work ethic is like no other. Once involved in a task, whether it is building a shed, carving or cleaning the house, he goes at it with all pistons firing, hardly taking a moment's break. If he doesn't know how to do something, he will work out how by either looking it up on the Internet or simply diving in to the task, and enjoying the challenge along the way.

During my prep for South Georgia, Dean took on more tasks than I could ever have asked for. Thankfully, he is a whiz when it comes to learning how to work new gadgets and, like me, he doesn't read the instructions. When he purchased his first laptop, he dove deep into the caverns of its technological heart. Most people would learn just the basics: how to send emails, open up a Word document or play the card game *Patience*, but not Dean. He pulls the entire machine apart, learns the inner workings of it then puts it back together again.

And so he was my gadget guy, my technical hero, the man behind the blog. In addition to that, he is an organizer, the kind of person who actually finds satisfaction in clearing out your kitchen cupboards completely, or sorting through your jumbled closet space, or even attacking your basement that is jam-packed with stuff. He is a rarity who finds pleasure in going through it all, throwing away the broken, giving away the unused and grouping together the items you want to keep and placing them neatly into a labelled box. He could make money sorting out everyone else's crap. He has been called 'My handy-husband' by a happily married woman, while she stood next to her husband who nodded in agreement.

Although Dean is built of different calibre and at times didn't quite understand why anyone would want to paddle around some remote island in the middle of the South Atlantic to help save a bird, his support and encouragement never faltered. He kept me on my toes anytime I showed signs of wavering. When I strayed off track he steered me back on again and when I was drowning in the busyness of South Georgia, he would throw me a line. He was my steel hull in chaotic seas and I will be forever grateful. Departing for the expedition and saying farewell to Dean was absolutely awful.

During the two years we spent together leading up to my departure for South Georgia, we had gone through some pretty rough times. We skipped the customary 'beginning of relationship' honeymoon faze and jumped straight into the nit and grit of getting to know each other, learning about our differences and becoming familiar with the skeletons in each of our closets. When involved in a relationship, it can't help but bring out the rawness of our fears and insecurities. Dean and I had gradual ups and plummeting downs, yet in the two months prior to me leaving we had a breakthrough. It was as though there was a shift in our own tectonic plates which brought us closer together. Our walls were down, our guards were seated and our hearts were opened to let each other in. After all his support and constant companionship in the whirlwind of South Georgia, my fear, doubt, uncertainty and nervousness were kept at bay. On the day of departure, I had to let go of that security cover, step out into the world of my expedition and face the outcomes alone. For the first time in ages, I was without my *blanky*.

Chapter 12

What Am I Really Getting Myself into

South Georgia is one of the few places where you can't just fly to. There is no airport and no port. Although it hosts the most uninhabited regions of the world, it is still an island where you cannot simply show up and explore. Every visitor is required to receive permission from the British government and the only way to get there is by an oceangoing vessel, a specialized boat built to withstand the most treacherous seas and ferocious wind, of the hurricane force kind. An old sailors proverb says – *"Below 50° there is no law, below 60° there is no god."*

Like your shadow on a sunny day, the wind is with you always in South Georgia. The fact that albatross nest there, the bird whose existence relies entirely on the prospect that the wind will continue to blow, wind is a given. It is the kind of wind that is impossible to prepare for. It is as unpredictable as my very fine hair in the morning. The wind can come from anywhere and at any time. It can blow you over with absolute ease, taking all of your belongings with it, including your only means of shelter. It is the type of wind that can cause even a large ship to drag anchor, thrashing it against the rocky shore in a matter of minutes. South Georgia is also cold, biting numbing cold.

South Georgia remains relatively unexplored (topographically) because of its remoteness and inaccessibility. Up to 1982, very few people had reached the interior of the island. A noteworthy exception was of course Sir Ernest Shackleton in May 1916, when he crossed the island to bring rescue to his men stranded on Elephant Island. It was not until 1928 and 1929 that Ludwig Khol-Lars and his wife sledged up the Neumayer Glacier to the Lars Plateau. The British Explorer, Duncan Carse did four South Georgia surveys in the years 1951/52, 1953/4, 1955/6 and 1956/7 which opened up the island to the possibility of serious exploration. His travel was by backpack and hauling sledges. He discovered two major sledge routes from Cumberland Bay East to Drygalski Fjord in the southeast as well as Cumberland West Bay to Ice Fjord in the far northwest. The maps used today are based on the results of these surveys.

Major climbing expeditions followed. Lieutenant Commander Malcolm Burley with the Royal Navy led a Combined Services team which retraced Shackleton's route and made the first ascent of the highest peak, Mount Paget, in 1964 and again in 1965. They also pioneered a high-level sledge route from Gjelsted Pass down the Lancing Glacier, across the Christensen and up the Kjerulf to the head of the Christophersen Glacier. On the way back from Mount Paget they climbed Mount Sugar Top and were the first to do so. Stephen Venables, a well-known British mountaineer, made the first ascent of Mount Carse in the Salvesen Range in 1990. He was forced to spend most of his month-long expedition in a snow hole because of ferocious weather they experienced. A skiing expedition led by Angus Finney that included South Georgia's Marine Officer Pat Lurcock, skied the length of the island in the year 2000. Each year, one or two parties attempt the Shackleton crossing; some are successful.

Up until 2005, there had been two attempts to kayak around the Island of South Georgia. Both efforts were unsuccessful. The first departed on the 18th of September in 1991. The *Royal Anglican South Georgia Expedition*, made up of four men, set out from Grytviken in extremely cold conditions. Heading in a clockwise direction, they paddled south for fifteen days, making little headway due to the tenacious winds that blew directly at them. It seemed they had underestimated the time it would take to complete the expedition as well as the inevitable delays caused by typical South Georgia weather. This miscalculation caused them to run so low on food they were forced to supplement their diet with local cuisine. What had once been a wildlife feast for their eyes, turned into a wildlife feast for their stomachs. Yes they succumbed to eating penguins.

"Once we tasted the meat and got full stomachs, the barbarity of our actions seemed justified. All in all a very satisfying discovery for everyone but the penguin," an expedition member wrote in his journal. But their situation soon became dire. They attempted to round the southern tip of South Georgia Island but reported waves that were nine metres high, causing them to retreat back to the beach they had been stranded on for over a month. Finally the Royal Navy stepped in and attempted a food drop. The parachutes loaded with necessities were deployed over the camp and hung above them just out of reach. In good old South Georgia fashion a gust of wind caused the supplies to be blown half a mile out to sea. The provision mission had failed. On October 29th, they were finally rescued by an aircraft carrier and returned to Grytviken where they had set off from, six weeks prior.

The second attempt was an experienced trio consisting of two Australian men and one American. All three had strong kayaking and canoeing backgrounds and the Aussies had previously kayaked in Antarctica. It was early December in 1996 when they departed from Grytviken, heading north in an anticlockwise direction. After making good progress, they were then beach-bound for six consecutive days. As soon as the first sign of improvement in weather appeared, they decided to make the broad crossing of Wilson Bay. In choppy, confused seas, halfway across, one of the kayakers capsized in the dangerously frigid waters. By this time he was already 5 km offshore. It was a dire situation. A bombproof Eskimo roll brought him upright again. Two hours later they finally made it to safety.

Continuing on, getting deeper along the southwest coast, past the point where turning back would no longer be an option, they pushed on bravely. This section of the island is extremely exposed. There are few places to land and the bays and coastline are inadequately charted. Glaciers take up most of the shore creating terrain that is steep and uninhabitable even for the wildlife. The shallow bays offer no anchorage or refuge for any boat. The men named this coastline *The Killer Coast*. Eventually, a unanimous decision was made to abort the mission of paddling along the coast and head inland to attempt the famous Shackleton Gap. The west coast was too dangerous and the three agreed that it would be well out of their comfort levels.

This reminded me of Shackleton's conservative decision to turn back only one hundred miles short of reaching the South Pole on one of his earlier expeditions. He knew he did not have enough supplies to get him and his men to the Pole and back again alive. This decision saved all of their lives yet it was the hardest decision of Shackleton's life, telling his wife Emily later: *"I thought you'd rather have a live donkey than a dead lion."*

The island remains a popular destination for adventurers to test their skills against the harsh elements and challenging landscape. Expedition members, whether traveling over land or by sea, hold South Georgia in their highest regard. It is an island that requires the utmost respect from all who chose to travel there.

I was committed to the goal of attempting a first ever solo-sea-kayak expedition around South Georgia Island and it was time to depart from my home in Alert Bay and let go of the supportive embrace of Dean. Although I was keen, eager and more than ready to finally get this adventure underway, it was the toughest departure of my life.

Chapter 13

Taking the First Step

Like many journeys, the time and effort spent preparing and packing seems to involve the most work. Once under way, everything gets a little easier and the process of carrying out the journey is simple, and the part you know how to do best. Sitting on the plane and about to embark on an eleven-hour flight was the first time I had sat and done absolutely nothing in months. It was an enforced 'just sit there and do nothing' and I welcomed it. I kept myself fairly busy. I had numerous movies to watch and a little homework to complete. I had a mission to accomplish by the end of this flight – to work out how my new watch functioned. I had never owned a watch with so many gizmos before – a temperature gauge, barometer, altimeter and five alarms. It was quite the watch.

Sitting beside me was Beth-Anne Masselink, my support kayak person who volunteered to join the expedition only two months before departure. She had a winter with no work contracts planned and I was one kayak support person short. Her role was to take footage and photographs, as well as be the kayak logistics and communications person onboard the *Northanger*. Her repertoire of experiences and skills was an asset to the expedition. Not only had she participated in her own remote kayaking expeditions, but she too had kayak-guided in Antarctica. She knew South Georgia as well as I did. As a kayak instructor, a tour guide and a student counsellor, she embodied the attributes of the vital 'team player' the *Northanger* required. Her calm and gregarious humour was a welcome bonus.

Beth-Anne's frame is one that does not go unnoticed. When standing, the six foot, seven inch gorgeous blonde towers over most people, but unlike many other folk of similar height, she stands tall, erect and proud of the many inches she commands. Her wavy locks and nicely proportioned build seems to match her confident character. I was relieved to have her beside me. Although I did not know her very well, her reputation in the kayak guiding industry was solid, someone you could trust and rely on. I was thankful for her company and looked forward to getting to know her.

Many times I have flown into Ushuaia[14] when contracted to work aboard ships taking tourists down to Antarctica. Unaccustomed to having no work obligations, it was quite the novelty having only ourselves to look after. After retrieving our six bursting bags, we noticed the friendly, familiar face of Greg waiting behind the airport security doors.

I had briefly met Greg once before while working in Antarctica. Our ship was anchored in a bay nearby a small British Antarctic base called Port Lockroy. We were anchored only metres away from the red-hulled *Northanger*. Having an interest in sailboats and a curiosity for those who sail to Antarctica in small vessels, I slipped away from my duties and popped over to visit the solid looking sailboat anchored in the bay. Greg popped his head out of the hatch, smiling a forced smile; I realized I had just got him out of bed. After a brief but polite conversation I let them be and retreated back to my obligations onshore.

We loaded our bags and paddles on the back of an old truck and squeezed ourselves in the front bench seat next to Greg. It was a short ride to the docks where expedition sail-boats tie up and a trolley sat ready for transporting our gear to the *Northanger*. We passed an assortment of sailboats, all rigged for Southern Ocean sailing and a new formation of butterflies started swarming in my tummy. Inflatable lifeboats were stowed on the top decks, self-steering devices hung

---

[14]Southern Argentina.

from the stern and a generous collection of jerry cans was tied securely. The red hull made the *Northanger* stand out from other vessels and, despite the bright and playful colour, it looked solid and sturdy which comforted me. The butterflies settled. Here, alongside this busy dock was the fifty-four-foot vessel that would take us to South Georgia and back again. She is our home and the crew our new family.

Leaving our luggage on the deck, we climbed down the nearest hatch, arriving in the galley where the rest of the crew waited. It was a joy to meet Magnus, a twenty-one-year-old from New Zealand who in his first sentence used the unique expressions of a Kiwi. He said 'yonks' (a long time) and 'choice' (really cool man), words I had not heard for over twenty years. Magnus had a head-full of dreadlocks and was built stocky and strong. His sense of humour was instantly evident, for every comment he made was accompanied by a broad grin that tightened his eyes, making them twinkle with vivacity.

I immediately felt as though I was right at home, literally, because Greg too was from New Zealand. A few decades older than Magnus, Greg had a head of silvery grey hair. His sun-creased face revealed many years spent on the water or up on the mountains. He had everything an outdoor guy possesses. Strong hands, well-worn clothes and a face that tells stories of the far removed corners of the world that he had explored. Even though he has this strong appearance, one has to lean in close to be able to hear his quietly spoken voice.

Keri, Greg's wife, is from Canada and is also the owner and skipper of the *Northanger*. She beamed with friendliness and excitement and it was immediately obvious that she ruled this floating roost. With a mixture of accents signifying her habits of travel, her voice was ladylike with authority and direction between the layers of sarcastic wit. Built lean with strong working hands, this woman displayed energy and strength but there was also a subtle vulnerability about her that I couldn't quite put my finger on. Here we all were, a team gathered by word of mouth and similar interests, ready to take on the first ever solo-sea-kayak expedition around

South Georgia Island. This is really happening. We are here. It is time to get the expedition going!

On the *Northanger*, my nerves that had subsided during the plane journey came scurrying back. After four years of planning and preparing it suddenly felt that I was here at the bottom of the world, the gateway to Antarctica, and actually living this moment. Our journey was about to begin and the kayak expedition was only a week or so away.

There were still jobs to take care of and items to purchase. I needed to erect my tent in strong winds to establish a technique that would work for one person. My satellite phone, computer and tracking device needed to be tested and connected. I was unable to transport fuel on the plane so we needed to shop for *benzene blanco* (white spirits) for my cooking stove. The four days we had, which would have been plenty, got extended to eight. Keri went into hospital to have minor surgery. She required a few extra days to recover before heading out to sea. Although this seemed like a minor delay, it knocked me a little. When looking at the big picture, a four-day delay may cause us to miss a weather window which then could alter the time it would take to get to South Georgia. It may set my kayaking departure back four or more days and who knows what weather windows are made available or taken away with that slight alteration. I was obviously on edge and therefore reacting to these unexpected changes of 'the plan.'

One benefit gained from the delay was the opportunity to connect with Dean each day, giving him updates on our progress and intended departure date. It was a chance to share feelings and thoughts but at the same time our communication unsettled me. Seeing him on the screen, not being able to reach out and touch him or be held by him during this anxious time was tormenting. We both admitted that we had the desire for the expedition to be over and done with so I could be home again. These feelings were insane but they were real. I was about to head out on a sailboat to sail across the Southern Ocean where storms are frequent, and then kayak alone around an island completely bombarded with ferocious winds and treacherous seas. It was a risky endeavour. I don't mean to be morbid here but you just never know when you won't see your loved ones again. Seeing Dean on the screen during our final Skype call could possibly have been the last time we ever saw each other again. And so, our farewells were teary eyed and emotional. We deliberately avoided using the term *goodbye*; instead we said *see you later.*

It was the first time that I was part of an expedition that was comprised of more than just me. A team of people, hoards of safety gear and supplies, a fifty-four-foot sailboat and a large chunk of change were all associated with an expedition which I had set my mind to. It was a voyage that didn't just involve me. I could not simply make my own way to the 'put in' and jump into my kayak to begin fulfilling my dream. It was a collection of several working parts that had to be adjusted and tuned to work as a team. A well-oiled machine was required to make this expedition a success.

January 28th

My stomach remained a churning ball all week while we waited to depart from Ushuaia. Is it simply unsettled nerves, I wonder? I need to eat. I cannot pick at my food and lose weight, not here, not now, not before a big ocean crossing, followed by a vigorous kayaking journey in cold conditions. That in itself will zap my energy and eat away at my reserves.

► Paradise Camp - shared with kings

▶ the river of kings

▶ the meeting of kings

▶ king penguin parent and chick in beautiful South Georgia

▶ filming the kings

▶ reflections of a king penguin

► king penguin chick on top of the world - photo by Brandon Harvey

▶ capturing on film the very essence of South Georgia

▶ dining with kings

► home sweet home after a day's paddle

▶ making a cold and chilly landfall

▶ nosy neighbours

Chapter 14

Release the Lines and Away We Go

The dreaded Drake Passage is classified as the worst open body of water in the world. Easterly bound low-pressure systems steam-roll their way through the gap that is created by two massive continents – South America and Antarctica. Huge seas and wicked winds turn this more than 600-nautical mile crossing into one of foreboding danger. This unpleasant journey is the tax you pay for wanting to venture to this far-reached polar paradise. I have crossed the Drake umpteen times but always on a ship no smaller than a one hundred and fifty foot vessel. At times I was gifted with the Drake Lake where the smooth swell gently lifts our bow and gradually places it back down on the trough of the passing swell. The Drake Shake is a different ride. Entire bridge electrical systems have malfunctioned as high waves have broken the bridge windows situated on the sixth deck. Blue water can be seen crashing over the bow as the ship enters into the deeper realm of the sea, the belly of waves that stand ten metres high. Sailing to South Georgia on a fifty-four-foot vessel was going to be an expedition in itself and I was curious as to how I was going to endure it.

With the lines released and all items stowed for the open ocean crossing that awaited us, there was a sense of calm onboard. Warm sun and glassy seas offered a leisurely motor up the Beagle Channel, away from the city landscape of Ushuaia. Keri baked cookies and put the kettle on, Magnus read his book and Greg stood on watch while Beth-Anne and I devoured the scenes on either side of this narrow channel. When working on the ships this is a busy time. New passengers have boots and wet weather gear to hire, zodiac engines need to be worked on and passengers must be attended to. After eleven years of working these trips this was the first time I was able to marvel at the many sites of the Beagle Channel.

Pelagic Cormorants flew past in flocks of over a hundred and Magellanic penguins porpoised towards our bow, coming close enough that we could see their entire black and white torpedo bodies underwater. Our first sighting of an albatross was the most common specie, the black-browed albatross. With a wingspan of only eight and a half feet they were able to drift through the sky in the mere twelve knots that blew. By now we had the foresail up but the engine still pushed us along at a steady six knots.

In twenty-four hours I had witnessed all extremities of the Southern Ocean. During the final hours of my watch on our first day at sea, I observed an open ocean sunset on a ripple-less sea. I was able to watch the sun sink beneath the sea numerous times as the peaks of the swell rose and fell in undulating motions. During a small swell set, the classic spectacle of an inflamed ball dropping beyond the sea gave a whole new meaning to the term 'The Golden Hour.' Pastel colors bathed the canvas of the sky and an albatross soared, covering all corners of this crimson scene as though it was the resident artist. As the sky darkened, stars appeared sporadically and for the first time I noticed the Southern Cross, a constellation I recognized from home. The Southern Cross is made up of four stars and is shaped like a kite flying up into the sky. It was a sight I grew up with and it brought back memories of numerous nights spent stargazing when I was involved with the Scouts. For this journey, I decided it would be our guardian who will look over us as we travelled.

The following morning I woke up groggy from an unsettled sleep and joined Greg at the chart table. He was peering closely at the recently downloaded weather satellite image. "We're going to get kicked up the ass," he told us bluntly.

Looking at the wind-grid I could make out the numerous red arrows indicating strong wind and the images of heavy cloud that drenched the Falklands. This system was rapidly making its way towards us.

The day turned into one spent indoors. The deck was awash with white water as we ascended up and descended down, each wave causing gallons of ocean-born water to be continually dumped on us. Only Magnus and Greg would attend to the sail changes. They had to be attached to a safety line at all times when working out on deck. Soon fog closed in and the birds that had been our companion all through the previous day vanished. We suddenly seemed very alone as the building sea was all that surrounded us. We kept an eye on the radar from inside the boat, checking every fifteen minutes the conditions outside through a closed hatch that offered good visibility. Magnus, who had grown up on sailboats, was born with sea legs and although our appetites were gone, he whipped up a hearty vegetable soup on the frisky gimbaled stove.[15] We all understood the value of keeping something in our stomachs. The aroma of home-cooking filled the small quarters of the boat and awakened those that slept and sent some to the toilet, head first. We were experiencing unpredictable shifts in the boat and, as I wrote in my journal, my stomach lurched in sync with the boat, vehemently objecting to the soup. I had felt committed to keeping my blog regularly updated for those who were following my journey, but it was time to quit writing and lie down for a bit.

February 3rd

Ok, I won't do an update, I feel too queasy but real quick... We hoved-to[16] overnight, sailed with the wind in the early morning, hoved-to again coz the wind got too strong.

---

[15]Most marine stoves are gimbaled, which means they sway from front to back in harmony with the boat's movement. On a sailboat, a gimbaled stove situated along the port or starboard side will tip backward or forward, depending on the boat's tack.

[16]To stop a boat and maintain position by balancing the rudder and sail to prevent forward movement. Heaving-to is perhaps the most successful tactic for heavy weather sailing, but each boat has certain idiosyncrasies that dictate the settings.

Puking, feel like shit, feel trapped in this small space, but appreciate the sturdiness of the boat and that it is built for such seas, but I'm not really into it. My body is cramped, stomach sick and I can't eat or drink much but boy! it's an adventure. We are just getting smacked by this nasty system which is sticking around. The barometer dropped 14 millibars in 1 hour and 20 minutes, which is HUGE.

How vulnerable I feel bobbing up and down like a redundant cork with little or no control over my destination. For most of the day I avoided any intimacy with the conditions outside. But the moment I decided to record what is really going on outside, I was horrified at the scene I attempted to film. I was instantly brought to the reality of our vulnerability, aloneness and the limits to my control over my own life. I am completely relying on other people's skills, experience and knowledge to keep us alive and well. Ok so I did write an update.

Chapter 15

Dream in Jeopardy – Accident at Sea

An agonized scream filled the entire cabin of the *Northanger* as it lurched violently in the building Southern Ocean swell. "That is not good." The words spilled from Magnus's lips as he and Greg worked on the cabin floor, adjusting the vessel's drive shaft. In fear of what I might see, I nervously glanced up from the book I was reading. Kneeling on the floor of the boat, Greg desperately clutched at his wounded hand and stared in disbelief at the bone that now protruded from his index finger. The expression on his face turned to one of horror. Every crease reflected excruciating pain. He suddenly fell back screaming, now that he had seen the extent of the damage. The majority of his index finger had been torn from his right hand and the missing part was left floating in the bilge.

Before the accident aboard the *Northanger*, Greg and I had watched the barometer plummet. Rapidly building wind and sea were inevitable. As Keri knelt beside Greg, supporting his injury, urging him to stay calm and move to the galley seat, the storm pitched the boat violently. In any emergency situation the main priority, once you have stabilized your patient, is to seek medical assistance as soon as possible. But, sailing in the middle of the South Atlantic, that seemed a slim possibility. Because of the severity of the storm, it was unsafe to have any sails up; the wind was too strong and it would put too much pressure on the rigging and on the boat. Despite the feeling of urgency to get to help, we realized the storm was in charge. We simply had to wait it out, much against our will. To Greg's dismay, we reluctantly set the bow into the waves, kept only our reefed mizzen[17] set, hoved-to and waited.

With his wound wrapped and elevated, Greg drifted into a drug-induced sleep as we waited for the unruly system to weaken. Eight hours passed and the wind let up slightly. Immediately we sprang into action and set a course for the Falkland Islands. Magnus braved the storm on the outer deck and placed two reefs in the main. With our course fixed for the Falklands, we were now bucking wind and waves. Sluggishly we inched our way north towards medical assistance and mile by mile we drifted farther away from my dream.

It took us three days to get to Stanley, the capital of the Falkland Islands. As soon as we were tied up alongside, a government official came down to meet us. Keri delicately packaged and transported the severed portion of Greg's finger, joining Greg as he carefully climbed into the jeep. The customs officer agreed to take them immediately to the hospital, clearing customs along the way. Magnus, Beth-Anne and I stayed to tidy and reorganize the boat. Items had shaken loose and needed to be re-stowed.

Three hours passed until we heard news which was delivered by the customs officer who had greeted us upon our arrival. He made a special journey back to the *Northanger* bearing news that the surgery went well and that Greg's hand was stabilized. "Was the portion of finger any use?" I asked in hope. "Ah no, it was as useful as cat food," the customs officer answered without hesitation.

Throughout the journey so far, the diligent tracking device had been plotting our course. By now all those watching would have noticed the drastic change in our direction. Our deviation was extreme. It was obvious that we were no longer bound for South Georgia. I wasn't able to explain why at

---

[17]Mizzen: the aftermost mast that supports all the after sails. When the wind rises, a reef in the mizzen is also useful to balance the rolled up genny, a large foresail or jib that overlaps the mainsail.'

first. We were waiting until the surgery was completed and Greg was stabilized. Greg's mum and dad were following the blog attentively therefore it was important that we were discreet and delicate regarding the incident. It was crucial that Greg's parents found out what happened from Greg directly instead of through a blog entry. Greg's dad was critically ill at the time, and had been advised that he only had a few months left to live. While Greg arranged a flight back to New Zealand to be with his dying father, Beth-Anne and I stumbled (too many days at sea) into action to search for a replacement crewmember.

We established ourselves in the Narrows Bar, a family pub situated along the harbour front, half way between where the *Northanger* was tied up and the township of Stanley. A friend, Chris Clarke, whom I had worked with during an Antarctic season, was managing the bar. It was a novelty to find a friendly, familiar face in the middle of this recent episode in the expedition. Chris looked after us. Beth-Anne and I had lost weight during our seven days at sea so the first thing Chris offered us was a pint of Guinness and cheesy chips (fries with melted cheese on the top). We devoured them and asked for seconds.

I was eager to reconnect with Dean via Skype on the Internet, another service which Chris generously provided. Dean was the only one who actually knew what had happened, soon after the accident had taken place. He had called family members who would be concerned with the drastic change in course and wanted to set their minds at ease. It was reassuring to hear his voice and to be able to share with him the details of what went on. Obviously he was concerned about Greg's well-being, but at the same time, he was anxious to hear about my Plan B. I had no answers but reassured him that we were on the search for a replacement crewmember.

Chris knew of a guy who had arrived in the Falklands by sailboat, after having single-handedly sailed large portions of the oceans. His next stop was South Georgia. Could he be our potential replacement? He was due to be in the pub later that evening, therefore it was in our best interest to stay in the pub a few more hours. Eager to speak with him when Chris gestured to us that he had arrived, we approached him like fans would a rock star. We cut straight to the point, sharing with him briefly what the expedition was about, the albatross cause and our recent mishap. He said he would give it some thought and agreed to meet us at the *Northanger* the following morning. Beth-Anne and I were ecstatic and skipped our way back to the boat, eager to tell Keri of our delightful discovery.

Talk about peeing in our cereal. Keri didn't like the man before even having met him. She didn't like anything about the idea. She pooh-poohed every positive aspect we gave her, making us assume that even if the most suitable candidate came along, he or she would not be good enough for Keri. It was as though she did not really want to continue with the expedition and understandably so. The poor woman's husband had just lost half a finger. He was about to fly to New Zealand, leaving her entirely responsible for the sailboat and crew which is a rarity with this dynamic duo that are a team. If this was the case, if she felt unwilling and unable to continue to South Georgia, despite having a suitable replacement onboard, we needed to know this truth, so I could then begin letting go of South Georgia and salvage the expedition by coming up with a Plan B.

February 13th, Stanley

It has been over five days since I last wrote in my journal. A lot has gone on, many things have been discussed, numerous people have come into our lives and emotions have been felt, expressed and shared by our crew. I have spent most days away from the boat. There is very little for me to do there. And so I venture off for most of the days to get things done. Dean and I have spoken daily, sometimes twice a day, as now I have access to call his cell phone using Skype. Beth-Anne has been my sounding board and level head although I have recently noticed that she could be getting worn down from it. She is getting it from both sides – from me and from Keri.

People have been amazing sharing their comments and quotes on my blog, which has offered words of wisdom, encouragement and comfort. What an asset the blog has turned out to be – for me.

Chapter 16

Life in the Falklands

Throughout my stay in the Falklands I felt as though I was in constant limbo. I was stuck in the middle of my disintegrating Plan A and a developing Plan B. The single-handed sailor did not work out, but this didn't stop me from searching for others. Against Keri's will, I called the local newspaper and, to my surprise, they had heard about the expedition and were trying to locate me in hope of writing an article. The benefits of small towns; news gets around in a flash. I was interviewed by a journalist from the *Penguin News* and interviewed by the local radio station. A week later, our story, along with our search for an experienced crewmember was published and on the air for all of the Falklands to see and hear.

While we eagerly waited, I began a fitness regime, swimming laps at the pool and keeping my upper body strength up by rowing. I had rowed frequently while training in Alert Bay. The first time back on the row machine here in Stanley, my spirits were suddenly deflated. "What the heck am I doing sitting on a bloody row machine," I shouted out aloud in the empty gym. "I should be in South Georgia, not here in this gym!" The feeling of utter disappointment and negativity came back in waves, but what kept them mostly at bay were my thoughts leading to Plan B.

I would be the first woman to kayak solo around the Falkland Islands. This had never been done before and, even more importantly, I love the Falklands. In some ways, they remind me of New Zealand; green rolling hills speckled with grazing sheep, turquoise surf crashing on cream of wheat sandy beaches and dolphins and sea lions cavorting in the waves. What make the Falklands really special are the farms that have hidden treasures. Along the tussock hillsides which lead you to the opposite side of the islands, you come across sheer cliffs that plummet abruptly down to the sea. On these very cliffs are colonies of nesting albatross, thousands of them. The largest nesting albatross colony exists on Steeple Jason Island, situated fifteen miles offshore. 171,000 pairs of black-browed albatross nest there and, when the winds are cranked like usual, it is a sight to see.

This journey would be fabulous but one of a different kind. Although these collections of islands are remote and rugged, there are people who live here and farmers who farm here. It won't be as solitary and utterly removed from anywhere like South Georgia. The wildness here is interlocked with the folk who have chosen a life far removed from the rest of the world. This island will be kayaked around and I will have tea and biscuits with the locals along the way and it will still be for the sake of the albatross.

The friendliness and the generosity of the people gave birth to a new way of thinking as we lingered in the Falklands. Arriving as strangers one moment, then driving around in a borrowed jeep and taking a shower in a private home the next, our stay in the Falklands turned into a highlight of the expedition. Janice Dent, the nurse who looked after Greg during his brief stay in the hospital, was a generous soul. She lent us her vehicle, gave us free run of her home and connected me with her ex-husband who had kayaks I could probably borrow. Steve Dent invited me for a family dinner, offered his charts of the Falkland Islands and the permission to borrow a kayak. I felt charmed with good luck. I also found myself meeting with a sergeant from the Royal Air force. All dressed in multi-cam they walked me through their collection of what were once unexploded ordinance that were found on beaches not far from the town of Stanley. They showed me the charts which marked the areas I should avoid at all costs. Unexploded ordinance still lie around, thirty years after the war had ended.

The Falklands War was fought between Argentina and the United Kingdom and started on April 2nd, 1982, with the Argentine invasion and occupation of the Falkland Islands and South Georgia. Britain launched a naval task force to engage the Argentine Navy and Argentine Air Force and re-take the islands by an amphibious assault. The conflict ended when Argentina surrendered on June 14, and the islands have remained under British control ever since. The war lasted seventy-four days. It resulted in the deaths of 257 British and 649 Argentinian soldiers, sailors and airmen, and the deaths of three civilian Falkland Islanders. It is the most recent external conflict to be fought by the UK without any allied states and the only external Argentine war since the 1880s.

The conflict was the result of an ongoing historical confrontation regarding the sovereignty of the Falkland Islands, South Georgia and the South Sandwich Islands. Neither country officially declared war, and the fighting was largely limited to the territories under dispute. The initial invasion was characterized by Argentina as the reoccupation of its own territory, and by the U.K. as an invasion of a British dependent territory. Since the 19th century and up to this day, Argentina shows no sign of relinquishing its claim. The claim has remained in the Argentine constitution after its reformation in 1994.

Beth-Anne and I sat in the mess enjoying a lunch with members of the Royal Air Force. We stood out like sore thumbs in a room of multi-cam and experienced yet another novel adventure during this unexpected detour. I was touched by the people who, without hesitation, jumped in and offered to help make Plan B more tangible. Then along came Brian.

It was Saturday, February 15th, the day my South Georgia expedition was about to be officially terminated. We had been here for two weeks and, despite our efforts in finding a replacement crewmember, no one had stepped up to the plate. Back at base, Dean had received phone calls and emails from people who were willing to abort their lives and fly immediately to the Falklands to stand in for our fallen skipper, Greg. Although we were deeply touched by these gestures, the expense of flights and their infrequent arrivals into Stanley did not make those offers feasible. My dream had become a distant haze on the horizon, one I tried to reach many times. But obstacles just kept on getting in the way. It was left to my imagination; this dream of kayaking around South Georgia, the reality of it had disintegrated with every hurdle we encountered.

It was a busy morning but a sombre one. Greg was heading to the hospital for a final re-dressing and check-up, and then catching the midday flight out of Stanley. As we sat in the galley finishing up with breakfast, voices called to us from onshore. I poked my head out to take a look at our unexpected visitors. A middle-aged man and a petite woman were standing on the dock, alongside the *Northanger*.

"We read the article in the *Penguin News*," the gentleman announced in a strong British accent, not one belonging to the Falklands. "We are interested in talking to you further about it as I may be interested in joining you. That is if you are still looking for a crew member." My heart started to race at this sudden possibility, but I pulled myself back remembering Keri's ongoing apprehension about the topic.

The couple introduced themselves as Brian and Lin who had borrowed a jeep to come down to the *Northanger*. They didn't have much time and Greg had to get going. I offered to ride with them back to town so I could fill them in on the situation and to get to know them a little more and then ask if they wouldn't mind dropping me at the hospital so I could say my fond farewell to Greg.

Brian and Lin left Sussex in England in 2004 and sailed to the far reaches of our ocean planet. They ventured to northern Spain then crossed the Great Atlantic through the Panama Canal then traversed the Pacific to the far-flung Galapagos Islands. When you have sailed that far you may as well keep going, and so they continued on to the Pacific Islands, then further south to New Zealand and Australia. Finally, having arrived in Malaysia after four and a half years at sea, their longest crossing being thirty days, they decided to take a break from their sailing exploits. Lin was a teacher and applied for a teaching position in an elementary school in Stanley. Falkland Island Law allows only one person out of the couple to work, keeping work available for the locals. Brian and Lin had already been in Stanley for five months and, although Brian was keeping himself pretty busy with volunteer jobs, he was starting to get restless.

The following morning, as we all sat around the galley table, Keri explained to Brian and Lin the type of person she was looking for. It was important for Keri to let Brian know that she wasn't looking for a skipper – Keri was the skipper and would be the one ultimately responsible for keeping the crew safe and making the final decisions onboard. We required more than just a crewmember; we needed someone who could turn their hand at anything, from electricals to plumbing, sail changes to engine tinkering. Brian seemed well-equipped for all of that. Any sailing done on the Southern Ocean is not to be taken lightly and it is not for the faint of heart. It is where the winds are most fierce and unforgiving and the waters surrounding South Georgia are even worse. We needed someone who would remain calm in hectic situations and be able to problem solve through any mechanical breakdowns. Lin vouched for Brian's suitability and explained his calm manner and approach to the numerous problems and situations they had experienced while sailing for five years. It was obvious right from the beginning that Brian would be more than suitable.

Brian started sailing a nine-foot dinghy when he was a teenager. He has sailed most of his life and, when onboard with Lin, he is primarily the skipper. Lin loves being at sea, feels comfortable enough on board and she doesn't suffer from seasickness. However, she is not a sailor. One could say that Brian has done an awful lot of single-handed sailing but with a compatible companion onboard. He is practical-minded, can fix just about anything and has the smarts to problem solve 'boat issues.' He's willing to get his hands dirty, knows how to troubleshoot engines and electricals, and has a manner that offers a friendly, calm and likeable character, not to mention his delightful British humour.

As I drove them home after our meeting in a borrowed jeep and in torrential rain, I observed first-hand the type of person Brian was and this convinced me that he was the man for the job. I had two kayaks tied to the roof and the wind on the top road was horrendously strong. I could see the kayaks shifting with every gust which made me nervous. I pulled over to re-tie the lines, without any expectation of either Brian or Lin helping. I was quite happy to attend to the kayaks myself.

Before I had even gotten out of the jeep, Brian had jumped out ahead of me, keen as custard and eager to help. As I secured one of the lines I noticed that his line had a nasty knot that had been tightened by the shifting kayaks. I watched him patiently tackle the knot showing no signs of frustration, remaining calm despite the fact that he was standing in the wind and pouring rain, dealing with someone else's problem. He was entirely unfazed by his drenched state and, job completed, we jumped back into the jeep. I turned and smiled at Brian, thanking him for his help. Completely content and smiling back he said, "You are very welcome." Despite my approval, Brian still needed to pass through the gauntlet of Keri's expectations. Perhaps with Greg gone, she may be a little more open to considering Brian as a replacement crew-member, which would ultimately salvage the expedition.

Chapter 17

Returning to Eden – Dream Revived

As we sat in our cozy galley, a rack of lamb roasting in the gimbaled stove, a customs officer browsed through our passports and paperwork and questioned, "You are going to South Georgia right?"

"Sorry can you repeat the question?" I asked, having heard it quite clearly the first time.

"South Georgia is your destination, right?" he repeated.

"Yes! Yes! Yes we are," I announced joyfully, as a grin as wide as the Atlantic stretched across my face.

By 4:30 pm, we were officially cleared but still able to move freely about Stanley for twelve hours. We decided to celebrate our departure by having an easy (no mess and no dishes) dinner. I made reservations at 'our local,' the Narrows Bar, feeling good about bringing Chris some customers since Beth-Anne and I hadn't brought much profit to his pub despite the numerous afternoons we spent using the Internet and drinking only water. We invited all those who had helped us out, including Nurse Janice and her family, Sergeant Rob and his co-worker, Ken Passfield who had only just returned from assisting with an albatross survey in South Georgia, and of course Brian's loyal Lin. It was an evening filled with excitement and well-wishes and lots of food. Beth-Anne and I knew it would be our last sizeable meal for a while so no guilt was felt after two desserts and a plate of cheesy chips along with my double portion of lasagna. That evening I proposed three toasts:

1. To newly found friends
2. For fair winds and fine seas
3. To Brian (and Lin for letting him join us)

By 6:30 the next morning, with a well-warmed engine and the bumpers on deck, our lines were released and Brian steered us out of Stanley Harbour. As we motored out of the unusually calm harbour, Brian's wife Lin stayed at the dockside waving excitedly, her image getting smaller and smaller as the diesel picked up speed. There were mixed feelings onboard, those of excitement and apprehension. We were all excited to be finally on our way towards the original intended destination, but we felt anxious knowing that we would face the fickle moods of the sea once again. Beth-Anne and I had already taken our seasickness medication and would continue to do so in hopes of keeping that churning stomach at bay. It was crucial I keep up my strength and food intake because, as soon as we arrive in South Georgia, I would begin paddling almost immediately.

It wasn't long before we had our dolphin escorts back, riding our bow and stern wake, staying with us for over an hour. Now on autopilot with Keri on watch, Brian eagerly followed Magnus as he led him through the boat's systems. It seemed Magnus was enjoying the company of another bloke. I had been impressed with Magnus and the honesty he expressed when letting us know his comfort levels when deciding whether a replacement crewmember was necessary or not. Most guys his age would have been all macho about it, even if they lacked the skills and wisdom to take on such a task. But Magnus was honest. He knew his strengths and he knew his weaknesses and, at the same time, having worked with Keri for so long, he knew her weaknesses and strengths. As a team they were solid, but perhaps not solid enough to take on South Georgia with just the two of them in a role of supporting a kayak expedition. How lucky we all were to have another body onboard to share with the watches and pitch in with the duties, but also to have someone who actually felt more at home on boat than on land. That was our Brian and I will be forever grateful. Our seven-day journey, bound for South Georgia, had begun.

Gorgeous light came upon us at the end of our first day back at sea. A dense grey duvet of clouds covered us, followed by a slipstream of orange light which stretched like a rainbow across the distant horizon. The light softened, creating impressions of shimmering gold which dressed the ocean's surface like a silk scarf. A lone wandering albatross surveyed the sky, soaring silently in the distance – a welcome companion.

It didn't take long for the seas to steepen as the wind picked up and, just like the forecast suggested, our first storm was upon us. Here we were, back to heaving this way and corkscrewing that way, rolling to one side then rocking to the other. Although I was keeping on top of my seasickness medication and eating light meals fairly regularly, I was disappointed to discover the medications were not working. It would be another seven days of coffin-confined-iciness!

Before this sailing trip aboard the *Northanger*, I always thought I would sail to New Zealand from Canada and perhaps spend a few years aboard while I circumnavigated the world under sail. I even imagined doing that alone. Beth-Anne always thought she would take to the sea and work onboard a Canadian Coast Guard vessel. Those dreams and desires seemed so distant now. I staggered towards Beth-Anne's bunk to check on her. She was suffering terribly from seasickness and needed to stay horizontal to combat her misery. Like a corpse, her body lay limp; only the vessel's rocking moved her body.

"Are you ok?" I asked.

"I'm OK," she replied stoically.

"I've had enough," I continued. "I can't stand these tight quarters and the violent movements of the boat every time a wave hits. I feel like I'm in a coffin and it's driving me bonkers!"

My words seemed to open up further dialogue between Beth-Anne and me. My complaining gave her the freedom, in some way, to voice what she was actually thinking and feeling. We both reluctantly decided that sailing was not for us. We were not built for living in such cramped and confined spaces, unable to run, jump, stretch and move about. Half in jest, we even confessed to our desire to give up totally on our adventurous lifestyles. We announced that, upon returning to Canada, we would both delve into a life where having two kids, a garden to putter in, and watching movies would be the extent of our adventuring.

At that moment, I would have done anything to be sitting in my kayak, going at my own pace, stretching forward, placing the paddle in the water and propelling myself onward. Instead, onboard now I slept like a carcass in my coffin of a bunk, my life in someone else's hands, and the pitching and rolling sea felt like my only destiny.

February 19th (3rd day at sea)

I lay in my bunk last night, unable to sleep as we got slapped and slammed by every third wave. I clung to my bunk waiting for the boat to completely turn over and pulled under by a freak wave. I realize it is my lack of experience which makes me not really understand the normal movements of a sailing boat. What is OK and what is danger? Beth-Anne was nearly flung from her bunk by a wave that hit, and sent a bowl which she held flying in the air then to the floor.

I'm feeling impatient, intolerant, not liking this confinement. My body is cramped, my unused muscles are deteriorating. I truly wish I could hibernate during these days at sea and be woken up when we get there. Kind of like what Beth-Anne is doing, smart lady. At the moment our speed is only 2 knots as we are in a hove-to position and have been for 18 hours! We are simply bobbing around the sea and drifting in the wrong direction. I try to tell myself – "Hayley, we will get there in nature's time, in nature's way." I have lived by that motto for years, yet the intolerance I feel for nature right now, holding us back, slowing us down, is extreme. "Forgive me nature for I am impatient with you at this time."

Brian feels so at home in these conditions. He is doing great, adapting to the boat, getting to know the navigation systems, but he struggles a little with Keri's controlling ways. She reacts strongly to every question he asks, as though she is threatened by them, instead of appreciating his interest and his wanting to know. I wish she could trust him and make the most of the strengths he brings onboard instead of reacting so defensively towards them.

As I passed the camera to Brian I explained, "Ignore my silly actions, just keep the camera steady and film until I ask you to stop, ok, cool, thanks Brian." With my harness attached to the safety lines I made my way to the bow and faced forward. I kissed both my hands then spread my arms out to the sides, blowing a kiss towards South Georgia. Yes we had land ahead, the mountainous, rugged, glorious snow-capped peaks of South Georgia were only a day's sail away. I could not contain myself. I continued to dance on the decks, dancing with joy as I celebrated having come this far. Brian grinned behind the camera. Although we could see South Georgia we still had a day of intense navigation as we ran through the iceberg obstacle course.

That night, having encountered numerous icebergs which weren't showing up on the radar, we decided to stop for fear of colliding with any ice. Instead, we drifted for the night, leaving a person on watch to check outside regularly and keep a close eye on the radar. The bioluminescence was an unexpected gift. Any movement (hard not to have movement in the Southern Ocean) caused the ocean to sparkle like a swarm of horse flies underwater. As we did, icebergs drifted in the currents, passing us like silent trains, some over seventy miles long. Thankfully, the weather was calm. The conditions were perfect for paddling.

Pulling into Grytviken aboard the *Northanger* felt like a triumph in itself. I felt the novelty of arriving on my own accord, with no responsibility for one hundred other guests and their vacation. This was my very own personal voyage, an expedition designed by me, the one responsible for bringing together this group of strangers who are all reliant on each other, like a family.

Thank you, Northanger, *for I am here.*

Having landed many times on tourist ships, I knew the King Edward Point base commander, Pat Lurcock. His familiar face was a welcome sight. He had been following my blog and knew the challenges we had already faced. He too was happy that we had finally arrived. One of the first things he mentioned to me was how miserable the summer had been. Hayley, even if you had made it here on time, you wouldn't have been able to paddle. There has simply been too many storms. They were experiencing one of the worst summers on record.

I was eager to move through the arrivals and customs procedure and Keiron Fraser, the other government official, was efficient as he took us through the environmental procedures we were required to follow while travelling around South Georgia. What was on my mind was my kayak. I was eager to be reunited with it and begin getting it rigged and packed for my long-awaited journey.

Keiron led me to the storage hut where my kayak was stored. Dean and I had wrapped it securely in Victoria a year ago and it was still wrapped, looking like a giant Christmas parcel. It had been shipped from Victoria, B.C., to Halifax, Nova Scotia, by truck. While investigating the best option to get it to Halifax, it seemed a truck was the only way. When seeking advice about the packing and transporting of a kayak, I was given contradictory advice. "A crate is the only way to ship a kayak," one expert suggested. Another expert said, "Don't ever use a crate no matter what. It needs to look like a kayak so the guys know what it is. That way they won't stack all sorts of other items on top of it, like they would with a crate." Dean and I wrapped blankets around it and used support ribs for the vulnerable areas then bubble-wrapped the heck out of it. After a cling-wrap finish we reluctantly sent my expedition kayak on its way. From Halifax it was loaded on to one of the ships I often work on which was heading to South Georgia. The crew onboard the *Akademik Ioffe* had gained respect for me over the years and they knew it was I who owned the kayak; they also knew its purpose. It was in good hands.

I unraveled it like a kid at Christmas and felt as though I was being reunited with a long lost friend. This kayak I had got to know well. Prior to the expedition I had tried out numerous kayaks and it was this *Looksha IV*, kindly donated by Necky Kayaks which felt like the perfect fit. It was lean and fast on the water but with ample space to carry a fair amount of gear. It was light enough to carry and strong enough to withstand the occasional collision with ice or rock. I had fine-tuned my Eskimo roll in this loaded kayak and the mounts for my video cameras had been designed, securely mounted and glued on to the bow and the stern by a shipwright friend of mine. We were a compatible pair and this was the kayak to take me around South Georgia.

I could not believe my eyes! How can this be! My kayak was destroyed. As I removed the bubble-wrap around the bow I discovered a seven-inch crack on the top deck, deep enough to expose the insides of the kayak. I continued unravelling it further only to discover there was more severe damage. A metre-long section of the deck had completely separated from the hull. There were ten gel coat fractures on the bow and stern and four holes right through the hull. What on earth had happened to my kayak? My heart sank at the evidence showing that my kayak had not survived the journey. In disbelief that this damage had occurred, I sank to the floor with my head in my hands. With all my guards down, unashamed of showing emotion, I sobbed like a child unrestrained.

February 25th

There was a seasick hefalump which snuck into the ship's cargo hold in an attempt to seek the steadiest part of the ship while transiting the South Atlantic in huge seas. The ship suddenly lurched, which caused the 10-ton hefalump to be flung up into the air with all four feet completely off the ground, then flung through the air landing on the starboard side of a lovely yellow Necky kayak. The angry hefalump got mad and, attempting to get even, took the kayak by its trunk and flung it across the cargo hold, where it smashed against the bulkhead of the steel hulled ship, causing the kayak to then land on its starboard side.

We all pondered about the events that had caused such tremendous damage to my kayak. Some of the possibilities were a little more realistic than others. I was sure it had happened onboard the truck bound for Halifax.

Although I had arranged a back-up kayak to also be delivered by the *Ioffe*, it was an okay second choice. With less volume, all my gear was unlikely to fit, and it was a kayak I wasn't as familiar with. When taking on such an expedition you really want your shoes to fit. I was unsettled at the thought of having to use my back-up kayak, but there was no other option.

The following day, Magnus and Brian decided to bravely attempt the repairing of my Necky kayak while Beth-Anne and I rigged the other kayak ready. I took my back-up for a test paddle, directing my bow towards the gravesite where Sir Ernest Shackleton is buried. It was the day to visit Sir Ernest and get a little perspective on my expedition thus far. Surrounded by the mountain range that frames the abandoned whaling station of Grytviken, I knelt beside Shackleton's granite gravestone and read the inscription on the back. *"I hold that a man should strive to the uttermost for his life's set prize."*

My prize – after investing four years of my time, going deeply into debt and doing many months of training and research – was this island, the spectacular island that despite its savage reputation, cast a spell over me ten years ago. Here I sat in South Georgia, alongside my hero, sharing space with fur and elephant seals, at the starting gates of my dream.

Magnus first visited South Georgia as a thirteen-year-old onboard his father's sailboat. He remembers roaming inquisitively through the abandoned whaling stations, being mesmerized by the whale-sized elephant seals and building from scratch a fibreglass snowboard. It was this handy-man approach that made Magnus not hesitate for a moment when deciding to repair my kayak. Although I had fibreglass, resin and epoxy to fix fairly big-sized cracks and holes, I didn't have enough to essentially rebuild a kayak. With the contributions from the *Northanger*, the research base's bits and pieces, and my stores, we had enough to give it a fairly good go. It would take at least five days. I was already three weeks late in starting; I could not wait any longer. I was simply running out of time and weather. I would depart the next day in my back-up kayak and the *Northanger* and I would rendezvous and do a switch in a week's time.

February 27th

Today was sensational! I was completely blown away, chuffed, pleased and extremely thankful as I observed this gathering of strangers coming together to make miracles happen. It was a day of craftsmanship, cohesiveness, hard work and it was highly productive.

Beth-Anne and Magnus tackled the continuing saga of mending my dear Necky Kayak. After a day of gluing, fiber-glassing and sanding, it actually now looks like a kayak again. In fact it has gained character. It looks hardy, rugged and has a 'don't mess with me' appearance. One of the base staff, Matt Holmes (on his day off) somehow got roped into helping Brian set up a mount for my 'Hero' High Definition camera. A fancy, multi-functional mounted brace was designed and engineered. Keri spent the day baking and roasting to feed the troops as well as preparing the boat for our departure. I rigged my back-up kayak, fine-tuned my gear, filmed a little and removed my expedition gear from the Northanger. It was time to move out of my cozy cabin and move to the great outdoors.

Although there was a nasty weather system approaching, presenting forty-five knot winds and five- to six-metre swells lasting up to three days, I felt the need to get going. Even if I paddle for one day and have to hunker down for three, at least I would have begun my journey and initiated my new life of living amongst the elements. It was time to expose myself to South Georgia, embrace the wilderness and begin listening, watching and feeling the natural rhythms of this special place and learning its many intricate ways. In the words of Graham Charles, a New Zealander, who with two others became the first to complete a kayak circumnavigation of South Georgia in 2005 – *"it is time to enter into the school of South Georgia."*

Chapter 18

Finally on My Way

On February 28th, the *Northanger* crew and KEP staff gathered on the beach and watched me pack, curious as to how I was going to fit all my belongings and gadgets in to the kayak. I wondered what they were thinking as I prepared for my departure. Some folk had already spent nearly two years living in South Georgia, while others, like Pat and his wife Sarah, had spent seventeen. They know the island like no other. They have gotten to know its charm and appeal to adventurers such as myself but they also have witnessed its unpleasant traits. Were they concerned for my safety? Did they believe that I would be successful? Did they feel the same doubt that plagued me, being three weeks late in a summer where the weather had so far been unreliable?

Dressed in my drysuit, my kayak laden with gear, I placed my pogies[18] on my paddle, climbed into the cockpit and secured my sprayskirt. Eagerly I pushed myself away from the shore. Cheers and good luck were called from the sidelines and a surprisingly well-coordinated Mexican wave[19] was performed by the KEP staff. I couldn't believe it. Here I

---

[18]Paddle gloves that fit over the paddle shaft

[19]**The wave** (North American) or **the Mexican wave** (outside North America) is an example of metachronal rhythm achieved in a packed stadium when successive groups of spectators briefly stand and raise their arms. Each spectator is required to rise at the same time as those straight in front and behind, and slightly after the person immediately to either the right (for a clockwise wave) or the left (for a counterclockwise wave). Immediately upon stretching to full height, the spectator returns to the usual seated position.The result is a "wave" of standing spectators that travels through the crowd, even though individual spectators never move away from their seats.

was sitting in my kayak loaded and ready for two weeks of travel. I am actually here and it is actually happening. I didn't know whether to laugh or to cry. In the end I did both.

One paddle stroke at a time, I inched myself further away from the support and encouragement on shore and the Mexican wave disintegrated. There on shore, one hundred metres behind me, stood a gathering of kind and friendly souls who had become supportive friends I would never forget.

Heading north out of East Cumberland Bay, each paddle stroke took me further away from Grytviken. I was alone. All I had to do now was concentrate and get this job done safely. Having been freed up from the recent company and busy-ness, it did not take long for my mind to start to race. My emotions were in conflict with each other. I was happy and relieved, yet I felt anxious and doubt crept into my mind. I had established this dream four years ago. I am now four years older. I questioned myself, "Will I be able to withstand the cold? Will I be smart enough to make decisions at crucial times? Will I be strong enough, wise enough and patient enough for what South Georgia will dish out to me?" Already I was feeling frustrated with the slowness of my boat. I so desperately wanted to make up for the weeks I had lost. But I knew South Georgia would not allow it.

The seas were unusually calm and the clear skies allowed the sun to generously warm my face. Icebergs scattered along the coast made it easy to mark my progress. The sounds from shore reached me even though I was a mile away from land. I could hear fur seals whimpering, and the swell of the ocean surged against the rocks. A black-browed albatross soared above me. Out to my right lay thousands of miles of vast open sea that separated South Georgia from the nearest land, the Falkland Islands. "This journey is for you," I called out to the albatross as it soared above me.

It was time to concentrate. As I paddled, I estimated the swell size to be one to two metres. Even though the air was still, it wasn't long before a lone black-browed albatross flew over me. I took it as an omen, my good luck charm for the first day on the water. I looked along the coastline I would paddle this day and noticed boomers on the horizon. I watched the occasional wave barge into the large erratic rocks like an angry bull. I looked out for kelp, an indicator of shallow water which would cause the swell to rise and break spontaneously. I watched a fog bank that was behind me and was curious of the direction it was moving. My memories of Vancouver Island came pouring into my head, remembering how quickly a fog bank could engulf me. As I paddled, I observed the shoreline I passed, taking mental notes of places I could land. I paid attention to the breeze that gently ruffled my hair, looking for signs of it accelerating. South Georgia's weather can change abruptly and I wouldn't have a moment to prepare. Winds can pick up without warning and cause the swell to build and the waves breaking onshore to steepen. At all times I needed to know exactly where I was and where I was able to go ashore. If headwinds suddenly hit and progress was no longer possible, retreating would be the only option.

I had not paddled for five weeks and after four hours in my kayak my lower back felt as though I was leaning against a blunt knife. With such calm conditions, despite the pain, I pushed on, passed my originally planned first campsite, arriving at my intended second. I liked how I was already making up for lost time. Leith Harbour offered suitable shelter from the storm that was soon to approach. I recalled the unsettling report from local sailors and those back at the KEP base who had warned me about this season. Storm after storm, blizzard after blizzard, little sun and regular snowfalls seemed the way of this summer. Having started three weeks late, I had only two weeks of allocated time to complete the full circumnavigation, which meant I needed most of those days to paddle. I had to be alert and ready when a weather window was made available, as this would be the only way that I could even come close to getting all the way around the island.

As I approached the shore I thought about the many chores I needed to do in order to prepare my camp. Having to film the expedition suddenly felt like an unwanted burden. "Film everything," Katie had said. "Even if you are exhausted and don't feel the need to, film!" As the fur seals reluctantly moved aside, I landed on a steep pebbled beach, pulled out my tripod and set my camera securely on top. Since the sun was out and the wind slight I might as well film the setting up of camp and get that over and done with, I thought.

It was late afternoon in the sheltered bay of Leith Harbour and signs of the incoming storm were already evident. Mares'-tail[20] clouds saturated the skies and my tent whipped about like a kite as I secured the guy lines to boulders. My body ached and I craved sleep but there were still chores to be done. I utilized the last of the sunlight and charged my batteries using my foldaway solar panel. I wrote an entry for the blog and sent a report to the *Northanger*. As I cooked dinner I looked through the day's video footage; it would be the last time I did that. Playing back video eats up battery power and I had to be conservative. In the confines of my tent, it felt surreal to be typing away on my mini laptop. This was my only means to communicate with the *Northanger* and Dean. I nervously watched my battery power decrease rapidly because of the cold conditions. In future I would write my creative blog entry on paper and type it in afterwards.

February 28th

Guess what? I have a sunburnt nose. Guess why? Coz I forgot to put sunscreen on while I PADDLED ALL DAY IN THE SUN, IN SOUTH GEORGIA! Yippee! I am on my way, I have begun and the expedition has started. For ten years I have been dreaming about this moment, for four solid years I have been planning and preparing for it. I am here, kayaking, camping alone in South Georgia and it is absolutely fabulous. I feel at home out here, watching the sea, the weather, the terrain and wildlife carefully. I found myself constantly examining my location in relation to my

---

[20]Cirrus clouds generally refer to atmospheric clouds characterized by thin, wispy strands, often bunched into tufts, leading to their common name of mares' tails

chart, paying attention to the slightest change from the wind and water. I have obstacles, challenges and glorious moments ahead. Thank you for helping make it happen. You know who you are! It is far from a solo journey, for there has been assistance, help, advice, support, other people's hard work and interest that has got me here, and you are with me and will be all the way. For you I will always be grateful.

Chapter 19

Beach Bound on South Georgia

In the past, I have landed and spent many a day in South Georgia but I have never spent the night. "What do the animals do at night?" I wondered. Do the juvenile fur seals stop frolicking along the shore? Do the blowing raspberry sounds that come from elephant seals cease to exist? Do the king penguins no longer trumpet call in the dead of night? It was a restless first night in South Georgia. The fur seals continuously wrestled and played all through the night and by 4 am a chorus of trumpeting king penguins was my wake-up call. The entertainment performed by the wild in South Georgia never ceases to amaze me.

As I unzipped my tent and took a peek outside the pebbled beach and nearby river, the rocks looked like a patchwork quilt. Snow had fallen, delicately obscuring the beach below and blending my tent with the snow-speckled mountainous scene behind me. I looked towards the outer coast and the gloomy scene was uninviting. White caps galloped northbound and the dreary sky merged with the grey stormy sea. I shan't be going anywhere today.

The rain and snow slashed at my tent and played havoc with the tent anchors. I filled my empty kayak hatches with boulders and placed boulders on top of my kayak. Having camped near a river, good-sized boulders were abundant and so I went about replacing smaller ones that held my tent guy lines with bigger ones. As an additional anchor, I attached my kayak to my tent. With all these boulders, I doubt I'll be going anywhere no matter how strong the wind gets.

I benefitted from this beach-bound day by testing out my communications with the *Northanger*. We discovered that there was a delay when sending and receiving emails and text messages by satellite phone. They hadn't heard from me and I thought they were late in sending an updated weather forecast. This was just another reminder that I am ultimately alone out here with only myself to rely on. It could be the best way to approach this expedition, to be completely self-sufficient with the limitations only coming from me. Perhaps this would be the more practical way to get the job done.

South Georgia is an island of torment. I battled the wind on the slopes above my campsite this morning as I attempted to take a short walk, in hope of getting a better look at the sea conditions on the outside. The first challenge was trying to avoid the fur seals. I either had to wade deep in the water to avoid the seals sprawled along the shore or climb high above on the tussock slopes to avoid the many that were scattered along the lower tussocks and upper beach. Even high up I stumbled across many as they were tucked beneath the peat lumps. They were camouflaged when either on the beach or grass and did not appreciate my sudden intrusion.

Once cleared from fur seals, I ascended the slopes rapidly as the wind pushed me forward, like I was a slave and the wind my master who had a whip, forcing me to go at speeds I did not like. At times I had to crouch low to the ground and thus defy the driving hand of the wind. Once I had reached the top I wasn't able to stand up – my frame needed roots to enable me to remain stable. The wind was too fierce. As I lay on my stomach, my elbows held firmly to the ground, I brought my binoculars up to my eyes. The water was literally being lifted up and into the air by the force of the wind and although the sun was shining and the sky clear, the three sheltered bays appeared like snow from the whitecaps.

Later in the day, an unexpected call came through on my VHF radio from a nearby ship. As an expedition leader (EL) onboard the ships, we have a schedule of the daily positions

▶ a wandering albatross preparing for flight

▶ blackbrowed albatross in flight

▶ albatross nest on islands exposed to relentless winds

► beak to beak - blackbrowed albatross

▶ blackbrowed near to fledging

▶ blackbrowed sleeping

► southern giant petrel after a day of scavenging

► southern giant petrel taking a nap

► navigational hazards - tabular icebergs miles long

► Lady Elizabeth ship wreck in Stanley Harbour

► eye contact with a wandering albatross

▶ wandering albatross have a 12ft wingspan, the longest of any bird

▶ the outstretched wings of a wanderer

► greyheaded albatross chick

▶ paddling in paradise

▶ the joy of journal writing in South Georgia

► South Georgia sunsets are like no other

▶ South Georgia reindeer

▶ curiously close with an elephant seal pup

► ice tow

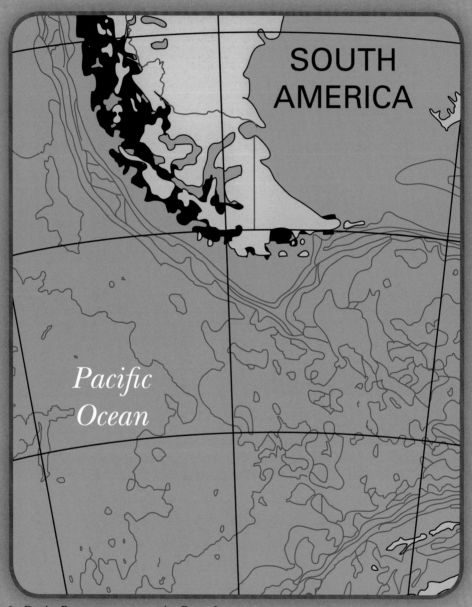

SOUTH AMERICA

Pacific Ocean

► Drake Passage - concept by Dean Laar

► sunset with the kings

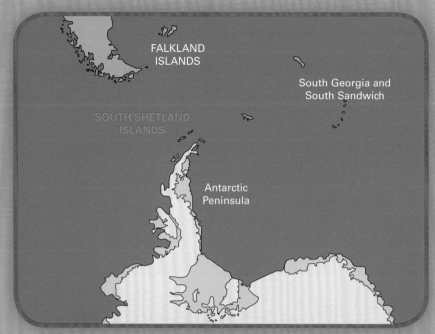

▶ map showing where South Georgia is - concept by Dean Laar

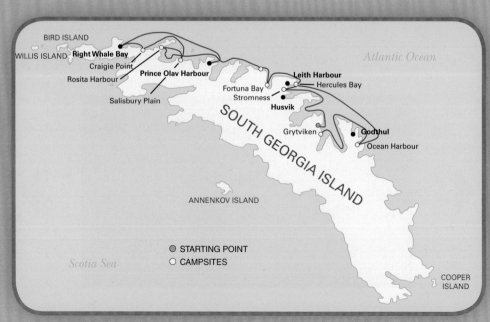

▶ South Georgia kayak route - concept by Dean Laar

of every ship in the vicinity. I had a copy of that itinerary. I knew the *Ocean Nova* would be attempting a landing in Stromness, a whaling station only two bays away from where I was camped. That afternoon I spoke with the EL onboard who happened to be a good friend of mine. He spoke of the hazardous seas they had just travelled through and the worst zodiac driving he had ever done. In some ways it was reassuring to hear how ugly the weather actually was out there when the decision had been made to stay put.

The following night the wind howled and struck at my tent more than the night before. Twice I went out in search of even bigger boulders to put on pre-existing boulders. It was unnerving watching my tent from the inside, changing shape completely, moving from a dignified half-hexagon to a distorted triangle. My curly locks will soon be straightened by the stress I felt that night. "Watch out elephant seals! I'll be tying myself to you soon."

March 2nd

Like clockwork, my tent lit up as it did the night before which again startled me. It was as though the abandoned whaling station had come to life by their night lights being switched on. But this was not so. My orange tent glowed like a candle flame and when I peeked outside to investigate, my head became drenched in snow and rain. I discovered who the culprit was. It was the moon, full as a pie which lit up the entire flurry of activity on the beach. I have recently discovered that the fur seals take their baths in the early evening. They twist and turn like a corkscrew whilst afloat in the shallows. Wow it is a noisy night as mums return from foraging at sea, calling out to their young ones, and the young ones calling back. Like sheep they take their turns blurting out to each other until they are side by side. I timed a pair once. It took forty minutes and seventy-seven blurts to be reunited.

I will see what the weather brings tomorrow and perhaps pack and be prepared to leave. Once on the water, I can at least poke my head around the outside and see how

it looks and, if need be, retreat to a nearby beach and es-
tablish camp if it's a 'no go.' Patience is the key, and plans
well thought through are the only way to go. From us here
at windy bay, the flurries and fur seals, I wish you well.

Few miles were gained the following day. I had watched
the winds all day yesterday and all morning today through
my binoculars, hoping for a break and an opening for my
getaway. My moment had arrived when I noticed a decrease
in whitecaps. I packed and loaded my kayak, and launched
around 1pm. It felt good to be in the saddle again but I had
to concentrate as the wind still blew strong and hard, more
forcefully than it had appeared from shore. It actually seemed
to liven up once I was on the water.

Twice, while in strong currents and frisky swell, my kayak
was snagged by a wave at the stern and I had to brace to gain
control again. I was intimidated but felt OK with my position
as I was fairly close to shore with some options of land to pull
in if I had to. I decided to attempt rounding Cape Saunders
and as I did the wind played havoc on me again. Whether it
was in my timing of being on the water or simply the con-
fusing seas, swell from the previous storm rebounded off the
rocks and katabatic winds charged down from the steep land
to my left which forced me to have to brace numerous times.
I glanced back from where I had just come from. All three
harbours in Stromness Bay were steeped with williwaws,
winds so powerful that they pick up gallons of water and toss
them vigorously onto the surface of the sea. They would turn
a kayak into a kite. To continue in these conditions would be
suicide, I thought. What awaits me is at least fifteen miles of
exposed coast with no sheltered bay in which to take refuge.
I thought it best I wait until the wind lets up to attempt this
stretch. I had seen a land-able beach not far from this headland and liked the idea of camping near the mouth of the bay.
That way I could keep a close eye on the very water I intended
to paddle once the weather and water was calm enough. An
hour paddled and only a three-mile gain. If I had to inch my
way around South Georgia, then so be it.

Chapter 20

Making Miles

It felt good to be on the water for an entire day, gaining miles and covering ground. It was the calmest day since setting off from Grytviken eight days ago, and I utilized it fully by seldom stopping to rest for the entire nine hours I paddled. I island-hopped in the Bay of Isles, relying on a compass bearing while I paddled in pea-soup fog conditions for most of the crossings. I was delighted to pass by islands familiar to me, where I had landed by zodiac, while working onboard ships. Albatross Island and Prion Island were icons that stood like cherished monuments. It is in this area, amongst the scattering of islands, where the wandering albatross nest. Due to the calm easterly winds that blew gently, I did not see one flying. Smaller albatrosses like the black-browed and the occasional light-mantled sooty albatross passed overhead as I paddled. There was a moment where my foggy eyes played tricks on me. I thought I was seeing a field of brash ice. Having seen no icebergs in the area, I wondered where the heck that ice came from. I soon realized it was fifteen to twenty pure white wanderers,[21] waiting patiently on the ocean's surface for the wind to blow once again. They require the wind to blow at least twenty knots in order for them to launch from a cliff or from the sea. Although this calmness is a burden for them, I cannot help but feel grateful that on this day this lack of wind was helping me.

Throughout the day I was frequently escorted by fur seals. They porpoised beside me and on occasion swam right

---

[21]Wanderer is simply another term for the Wandering Albatross.

beneath my hull. Giant kelp laced the rocky outcrops, seeming alive as the incoming surge from wind swell made them sway vigorously in the water like bundles of sea snakes. After five hours of paddling my back stiffened and my left leg went numb but I ignored the discomfort and continued on, happy to know that today I was making progress. I will sleep well this night.

It was the first day that the *Northanger* and I were able to communicate in real time over VHF radio. I needed to resupply my food provisions but more importantly it was time to exchange kayaks. Yes, my Necky kayak was repaired and ready to join me on my quest. Due to the most recent forecast and expected sea conditions, Rosita Harbour was an ideal anchorage for the *Northanger*. I was eager to do the exchange and so agreed to camp on a beach near the harbour where they will be anchored.

It was strange to be onboard the *Northanger* once again, so soon into the expedition. I had not been inside for nine days and nights and it felt like a barrier blocking me from the outside world to which I had become so accustomed.

Meeting up with the *Northanger* also gave me the opportunity to discuss the big picture for the coming week with the crew. Keri looked at the five-day forecast and once again it disclosed the probability that my progress would be restricted by high winds and rough seas. There was an occasional window of calm here and there, but not enough to get me around the northern coast and down the southwest side. Keri's talk of long-term plans and our tentative day of departure from South Georgia unsettled me. My stomach churned at the thought of not even rounding the northern coast.

I played with the idea of adjusting the international return flights I had purchased for Beth-Anne and me, to give me a bit more time, a few extra days to get around the island. However, upon meeting up with the crew I was told of a recent news broadcast which would end up being yet another factor that could potentially affect the success of the expedition. I was flabbergasted to hear that an earthquake had occurred in Chile the very day of my departure from Grytviken.

The airport we were supposed to fly out from was damaged, declared unsafe and therefore closed. Flights were backed up for at least three weeks. We needed to find a new way home.

In the big scheme of things, all these plans seemed irrelevant to me now that I was immersed within the womb of South Georgia, but realistically we had to plan ahead. Keri required a certain weather window to get us safely back to Stanley, and then on to her and Magnus's other obligations. I was not in the financial situation to lose the flights I already have and simply purchase new ones. I had limited resources and was faced with a reduction of time and inadequate weather. Since it was difficult for me to make new flight arrangements from my kayak or even from the *Northanger*, I once again leaned on Dean. He recruited a friend of ours to explore the idea of exchanging our flights for new ones.

That night as I camped in the pouring rain I had a companion. I invited Beth-Anne to join me for the night, figuring that she could do with a break from the *Northanger*. It was important to touch base with just her and without the distraction of others.

As expected things had been rather tense onboard and with Beth-Anne as my representative onboard while I paddled, she was receiving the brunt of the conflict and the pressures that Keri continuously placed on the expedition. It had started the first day I set off. My plan was to aim for Madison Bay, only a two-hour paddle away from Grytviken. With the weather being so calm and only a couple extra hours to the next intended campsite, that first day I decided to push on. Keri complained about me not sticking to my plan. Seizing the moment and making use of unexpected good weather was the only way to give South Georgia a go.

The second upset was when I inched my way to Hercules, when there was a brief break in a storm. The *Northanger* had decided to stay put in Grytviken and Keri expected me to wait until the *Northanger* was ready to meet up with me. That didn't make any sense to me. Why would I need to wait for my support vessel? Who is supporting whom on this expedition? We did finally meet up although Keri was reluctant to do so. I was dangerously low on battery power, including my satellite phone which was my only immediate communication device. The VHF radio had become useless due to the *Northanger* being over twenty miles away. They pulled in to Hercules Bay, stayed for a mere thirty minutes then departed.

Keri was frantic to get the boat anchored safely in Prince Olav Harbour. Even though I am now captain of my own vessel and the leader of my expedition, she still wanted to control me and my movements just as she had tried to do during my time onboard. "You can't sit there! You should tie your hair this way! You must wear this when you go ashore! You are NOT pumping the toilet thirty times"! On and on she would be on our back making us feel as welcome as a rat on HER boat. I couldn't help but question her choice in her profession. We all just seemed like a bother to her and a burden on HER boat. I was thankful to be away from the boat but I felt badly for those stuck with Keri's ridiculously controlling personality. I was starting to get the feeling that Keri was well over her head with this expedition. That was unfortunate as I felt it was hindering my success.

It was important that I put things in perspective. Here I was, kayaking and camping alone in South Georgia. Although the expedition so far had been racked with constant challenges, I am here and it is absolute bliss and I am grateful for Keri to have brought us this far to make this dream somewhat of a reality. Under the circumstances, we are all doing the best that we can.

When the wind let up and it was time to move on, Beth-Anne returned to the *Northanger* and I happily packed my Necky kayak. The imaginative staff back at King Edward Point base had christened it with the fitting name, *Banana Split*. I liked the new look. Obviously a paint job was not a necessity; therefore the blemishes and mended wounds stood out like the scars on Frankenstein. This kayak meant business; it had a bruised, but not battered appearance, one of solid stature. Good job Magnus. I owe that fella, big time.

Chapter 21

Battling with South Georgia

South Georgia makes you work for every inch of every mile. When the wind is light the swell is confused and the waves crashing on the shore are immense. A landing site may offer protection from the wind and a flat piece of ground but the fur seals may be extremely aggressive and territorial, limiting your movements on shore. Nothing is easy and, like a ballerina, you have to be on your tippy toes and in a constant state of paranoia. To let your guard down just once, to slip up an only time, the savage power of the island could destroy you. It would be easy for you to become just another bundle of bones, bleached by the sun and turned into just another fragment of South Georgia history.

Throughout my work on the ocean, I have come to realize that a weather forecast only offers guidance, giving me an idea as to what may arise. I take the information lightly and proceed with caution, particularly while traveling around this sub-Antarctic isle. It helped to watch my barometer and compare it to the weather texts I was receiving from the *Northanger*. It was important that I had an idea of at least one scenario that may occur the day I hoped to travel. I was still getting my hopes up when I received favourable forecasts and was soon disappointed when a perfectly suitable forecast was bastardized by the real weather that played out that day.

Having paddled for only two hours, the wind was starting to really piss me off. "What the heck are you doing here?" I shouted out to the open air. "Give me a bloody break will you!" I used my anger to propel myself against the strengthening wind and, while doing so, I glanced over my left shoulder at the nearby glacier which stood sheer and stark beside me. The gap between the face of the glacier and where I paddled was a mere seventy metres. This was a dangerous place to be.

At the same moment I realized I was making no progress. The winds that raced towards me were winning a battle I never agreed to fight. No matter how hard I paddled, my kayak remained stationary. This is the typical fashion of katabatic winds, which are gravity driven. They plummet down steep, narrow valleys, then blast out towards the sea. If it is a narrow inlet or fjord they are escaping from, the force is powerful and can easily take a less-powered vessel out to sea. The landing site I was aiming for required me to cross two openings of two fjords. That plan was soon abandoned. With momentum, the lively wind galloped southbound, hitting me like a heavy blow from a boxer. The glacier looked intact. I could not see any bergy bits floating beneath it and it displayed little sign of calving, but I still felt tense and eager to paddle clear of it. I thought about the four years and all the effort it had taken me to get to South Georgia. I refused to turn and go backwards. I was determined to push on. Watching the surface of the water and closely keeping a watch for wind gusts, I maximized the lulls and, one paddle stroke at a time, the glacier was soon behind me.

An assembly of rocks and reefs lay ahead of me which I hoped would offer some refuge from the wind. Instead, the wind roared through the obstacles as though they did not exist. At one time, my paddle was nearly blown clean away from my hands. It seemed the wind and weather was building. It was time to get off the water. At the northernmost point of the glacier was a moraine and directly below it a beach, large enough to hold at least three games of volleyball simultaneously. It was as good a place as any. The wind swell snapped at the beach and made for a messy landing. It felt good to be on shore but the feeling of relief was short-lived.

Just like the challenges South Georgia continued to throw at me, the wind refused to dissipate and it was a freezing wind. No down or Gore-Tex® layer could block the bitter cold which accompanied the screaming wind that penetrated through my numerous polar layers. I was soon cold, dangerously so, and needed to warm up quickly. With numb hands I fumbled at the hatch covers, trying to ignore the territorial fur seals who growled at me, their mouths wide, red and foaming like demented dogs. I threw on my puffy down jacket and decided to put up a shelter. With the tent tucked securely under my arm I weaved amongst the hyperactive seals that scrapped and scuffled. I was in search of a flat area, as well as shelter from this notorious wind. The only area suitable was not on offer. It was taken by a group of adult fur seals, aggressively scrapping and shedding blood as they did so.

Larger than mastiffs, and with lions' manes, the fur seals' heads were held high by their flexible, long front flippers. Fur seals have the right of way in this sub-Antarctic region, made obvious when they lunged towards me, teeth protruding in the act of a fake charge.

With no other choice and exposed to the wind, I settled for a campsite near where I had landed. I began to gather basketball-sized boulders for tent anchors. As though in the midst of a rugby game I tackled my violently flapping tent down to the ground and lay on top, holding it steady as I calculated my next move. While on my belly, keeping the unruly tent from blowing away, with a boulder in my hands, I crawled using my elbows inside the deflated tent and placed the boulders along the insides. The corners, burdened by weight made it difficult to thread the poles through the sleeves.

Forty-five minutes passed and the arduous task was finally completed. Sheltered from the wind that now thrashed against my tent, I lay exhausted on my mat. Instantly, I felt the stillness of air around me and welcomed the warmth that followed. During the night the wind dissipated as I drifted in and out of a restless sleep. Thoughts overshadowed my weariness. 'It seemed I had done a Shackleton,' I reflected. Shackleton was warned about the unusual abundance of ice in the year he set out on the *Endurance* expedition but he continued his mission despite the warnings.

I simply chose the wrong summer to attempt my expedition. It was as though the entire universe was giving me signs that I should not go. How many setbacks does one expedition need to have? I was starting to panic with the few days we had remaining. I had only got a third of the way around and this had taken me nearly twelve days. This measly progress was not going to get me around South Georgia.

During this night, I craved domestication. I envisioned Dean cooking a baked salmon dinner with roast potatoes and a yummy salad, ending the long and arduous day with a movie in bed, cuddling and munching on midnight delights. I felt vulnerable and teary-eyed this afternoon because of the reality of what this place can dish out, how quickly it can change and catch me unprepared. I am defenseless in this desolate place.

The occasional high-pitched whine from my fur seal neighbors and the harmonic tones of king penguins, chorused in a perfect rhythm, sent me off to a deep, slumbering sleep.

The following day, having received a decent forecast for the morning, I set off from 'boulder beach,' entering into a world of grey. The sky hung low and gloomy and the sea had the same tinge of dull grey. Plump snowflakes fell lethargically from the clouds which minimized my visibility of the shore. It was an eerie scene as my visibility lowered and an unexpected blizzard set in. I could no longer follow the coastline and look out for emergency pull-ins. It was as though the coast was hidden behind a curtain, and a faint silhouette of the land was all that I could see.

I was unable to gather the information I needed. It was a rugged shoreline, laced with numerous rocks and reefs that stood abruptly out of the water like giant jagged teeth. There were a few icebergs around and I wondered if they were the same ones we had passed on our approach to South Georgia two weeks ago. I tried calling the *Northanger* on the radio. Surprisingly, they answered and stated that they were at anchor in Right Whale Bay. I was on my own, as usual. The heaviness of the sea and sky, the doom and gloom of the mountains and rocky cliffs concealed by the blizzard, intimidated me. It was an unwelcoming scene.

It didn't take long for the blizzard to pick up its pace. I was now paddling blind as the snow penetrated my eyes like razor blades, stinging with every innocent flake. I held my head down, occasionally glancing up to check my bearing. The squalls were arriving more frequently and I soon realized they were coming from the west/southwest. Particularly nasty weather comes from the west in South Georgia. I was hoping to round Craigie Point, my last headland before reaching Right Whale Bay. When the visibility lifted a little, I noticed a beach with little swell; I made note of it, just in case the conditions worsened. I paddled on, gaining very little ground as the gusts lingered and the squalls were constant. The 30-knot southwest wind was not forecasted until the afternoon; it was only 10:30. I turned my bow and aimed towards the bay. The direction of wind was now land borne, displaying the typical characteristics of katabatic winds. They screamed down the valley, hitting me with a familiar force. I gripped my paddle, leaned forward and paddled hard into each squall; it lasted an eternity. I could not stop paddling, because if I did the wind would push me so far back so quickly, my efforts would be wasted. Once again I had been forced ashore, only to spend yet another night with the company of a wicked wind.

March 12th

I am here, experiencing South Georgia intimately, witnessing the varied wind and sea conditions. I am becoming familiar with the land and its contours, noticing the sudden change of temperature, the clouds and sea state.

I am here alone watching closely for a window of opportunity I can grasp and make good use of. At the same time, my mind questions what potential dangers I have around me when I want to land or camp. How will the wind affect me and my tent in this area – is it in the safest place? Winds play havoc because they rebound off everything – valleys, mountains and out from the bays. You name it – the wind is blasting off of it. It can be blowing from one direction but as soon as it hits an obstacle and bounces off another, the direction changes. You are never safe from the wind in South Georgia.

Every day I share this gorgeous place with wildlife that seems rather tolerant of my intrusion. The energy and moods of the wildlife varies at each campsite. The communities of animals, although they are the same species, interact differently with each other and with me. At some sites the fur seals ignore me completely; at others, they are constantly by my side, watching me, lunging at me as though they don't want me to pass.

With all of this – I have come to realize that I could do this. I could succeed with my goal and accomplish what I originally set out to do. All it requires is time which I and the Northanger are unfortunately running out of. This thought is tormenting me a little, so right now I am putting it out of my mind and trying to be in the present. South Georgia is good for that. It is the one place that forces me to pay attention and be in the present; otherwise I may miss things, or make a mistake that could cost me my life.

Chapter 22

Shore-Bound Moments

Cellular phones, Blackberries, laptop computers, Skype and other Internet communications have kept us continuously in touch with each other. Rare is a moment when no one can get in touch with you or find you for that matter. It is as though we are technologically connected to one another and under constant surveillance.

The remoteness and potential dangers, not to mention the governmental laws throughout this particular expedition made gadgets a necessity. Usually I tend to keep my gismo-world pretty simple. For the longest time I refused to exchange my pager for a cell phone. I still own tape cassettes and enjoy listening to them on my Walkman and I don't have the slightest clue how to use a remote control for a digital T.V. This lack of 'mod cons' did not however, interfere with my enjoyment , or rather the novelty, of having a good old chat with Dean on my satellite phone as I sat beside my tent, surrounded by king penguins, on a beach in South Georgia. I was grateful for my gadgets then. I had just finished 'dancing with the penguins,' literally.

"Are you sleeping OK? Are you warm enough? How are your wrists holding up?" were some of the thoughtful (and cute) questions Dean asked me during our two minute phone call. It had been a rough day and I needed a 'pick me up.' Having replaced my Walkman with an MP3 player for this trip, I had asked Dean to select tunes for my expedition. As I stuffed the earphone buds in my ears, I selected a file that was entitled "Upbeat Tunes for Hayls." As the music filled my ears which had only been listening to the sounds of nature for weeks now, I went instantly back in time to the mid-80s as Pat Benatar sang *I Got Brass in Pocket.* I couldn't help myself – I felt the desire to dance and I did not hesitate.

'Dance like nobody is watching,' someone once said. Well I have about four hundred pairs of eyes on me, six hundred if you include the skuas and sheathbills. Fur seals followed me, king penguins strutted towards me as if wanting to join in with the fun, and lethargic elephants raised their heads for a brief look. No doubt about it, neither of these animals had witnessed such shenanigans, nor had I indulged in any quite like it.

That evening it was a rare occasion to be able to sit comfortably outside my tent; most days it was simply too cold. This evening the weather was fair and it was time to pamper myself. I unraveled my knotty braids and combed my hair thoroughly. The comb felt good on my sensitive scalp. I washed my face and my neck with baby-wipes and rubbed moisturizer in my hands. As I glanced out to sea, enjoying my relaxed state, in disbelief I noticed I had a visitor. A zodiac was approaching the shore with someone in it. "Who the heck is that?" I questioned. "And what is he doing on MY beach?"

My solitude dissolved as this stranger, dressed in a mustang float suit, approached me. He had pulled the black, five-metre zodiac slightly on shore. As I made my way towards him I stopped, flabbergasted. "Captain Nikolai, what are you doing here?" I knew my visitor. He was a captain I had worked with for years on an expedition ship.

In a strong Russian accent he explained, "I was in bridge, going to Fortuna Bay and saw orange shape on beach. Through binoculars I could not know what it is, so after we drop anchor, passengers now eat, I take zodiac to investigate."

While I told him about the expedition and showed him my tent and kayak, I watched the waves breaking on the shore. The tide was dropping and I feared that his zodiac would soon be beached. I mentioned my concern to Nikolai but he did not seem worried at all.

I have spent many a time pulling beached zodiacs off the beach but always with five or six others to help. The zodiac is laden with two 25-litre fuel tanks and a forty-horsepower outboard engine, not to mention the safety barrel and anchor. These boats are bloody heavy. I did not feel like company for the night, particularly that of a Russian captain who was out of VHF radio range from his ship. I pointed out the zodiac to him again and this time I ignored his carefree response, "It is OK, no problem."

We stood on the beach beside his zodiac, keenly watching the swell sets arriving onshore and the incoming waves going nowhere near his zodiac. He finally realized the reason for my urgency. As a larger set approached, we grabbed the lines and pushed the boat. Like a beached whale it refused to budge. We tried a few more times and had some success in moving it slightly. I needed to change into my drysuit so I could wade in deeper and not be limited by having to stay on dry land. I ran and grabbed my drysuit and just as it was mostly on, a big swell set presented itself and it seemed this would be our only chance. I ran down the beach not bothering to finish the job of zipping up my drysuit.

We heaved, pushed and pulled with all our strength as a big set rolled towards the beach. With the first wave, we moved it a little but not enough. These swell sets usually come in threes, so we had two remaining chances. The second one was a goody and the boat was nearly afloat. Just as the third was about to arrive I yelled for Nikolai to jump into the boat. He placed himself next to the engine as I pushed the zodiac that was now floating freely, released from the clutches of the beach. Nikolai tried to start his engine but could not. Without engine power, the surge was dragging him towards the beach and the wind was sending him sideways towards a nearby reef.

I was now chest deep in the water. Grabbing the lines I spun the bow around so the stern faced out to sea and gave it one last push. Finally his engine sputtered to life and he reversed out to deeper water. As Nicolai motored away I waved back at him, smiling but cursing him silently for being so inattentive. That was exactly the scenario that I saw coming, even before he had landed that zodiac on the beach.

I turned towards my tent and felt the adrenaline wearing off, then I felt cold water trickling against my skin. I suddenly remembered that I had not zipped my drysuit up properly. I was wearing my only clean set of bedtime clothes, and they were soaked. The inside of my drysuit was also soaked after having dried inside and out throughout the sunny day. I had to wear and paddle in a wet drysuit in Antarctica. That truly sucks! All because of a cavalier Russian captain.

My days on shore were none other than entertaining. Even while immersed in the daily chores of erecting my tent, cooking dinner or securing my kayak, the wildlife made every task eventful and memorable. Eyes were constantly on me and my equipment, as though I was just as much a novelty to them, as they were to me. I was followed and watched, pecked at and even sat upon. Every moment I cherished.

One wildlife encounter did concern me however. One tranquil evening, as the last of the daylight faded into dusk, a juvenile elephant seal, weighing I guess about 1200 pounds, swam in from the surf and landed directly below my camp. Like a giant worm he rippled his way up the beach, resting occasionally then continuing on until he was satisfied with his position which happened to be right beside my kayak. Minutes later it looked as though he was attempting to snuggle. He placed his pectoral fin up and over the top deck then positioned his chin on the same area.

When it seemed as though he was about to clamber on top of the kayak I objected. The poor kayak had already been busted by a hefalump, I'm not sure it could withstand another beating no matter how playful or innocent. That kayak, although battered and bruised, was my only wheels, my ride to get around the island. I encouraged him gently to 'step away from the kayak' by clapping my hands and gesturing towards him. Finally and somewhat reluctantly, he found a companion of the same specie to cuddle up against.

Chapter 23

Conflict when Sharing Dreams with Others

The success of my expedition wasn't just up to me and although I wished for this to be so, I knew it was not a possibility. I wasn't simply paddling around a local island off the coast of New Zealand or Canada. It was a well-removed sub-Antarctic Island with a colourful political state. South Georgia is an island well guarded and governed by a small body, yet it is connected to the major country of Britain. Permissions, permits and regulations are mandatory. On top of that, those brought together to support an expedition are also a basket of colourful characters and personalities. They are just as much a part of making this dream come true as the one who had the dream in the first place. These seeming contradictions often plagued me with frustration.

Throughout my life I have had difficulty accepting help from others, whether it is borrowing somebody's car, or asking to get picked up from the airport – any kind of favour really. I feel guilty when asking for help, feeling as though I am putting the other person out. What's ridiculous about all this is that I really enjoy being asked by people to help them. I willingly and eagerly like to help people out.

For this expedition I had no other choice but to accept help from others. I was forced to rely on a collection of people, equipment and logistics all needing to work together cohesively. If something failed or someone slipped up, the entire expedition could be in jeopardy. It did not matter how much time was spent on putting the expedition together or how much money was invested in it, nor did it matter that it was somebody's personal dream for an important cause. Someone or something other than me could change the course of the expedition. This was an aspect I found very difficult to accept. My stomach is doing flips as I write this, remembering the frustrations I felt when things were not going as I had planned.

In the way of a Buddhist perhaps, you simply have to embrace all challenges and setbacks. Blaming something or someone does not fix or solve the problem. It is just the way it is, so let it be. I like the principle and believe in it wholeheartedly. In my usual day-to-day life I probably could go along with it; however, the expedition was a bit different. I had so much invested in it, I found it difficult to watch it slip away. I obviously have a long way to go before I become enlightened.

While dealing with the challenges I faced throughout the expedition, it did not matter how strong-willed, how courageous or determined I was. If the team, equipment and/or logistics failed in some way, the outcome was out of my hands. Back in Ushuaia, the estimated time of departure was delayed due to reasons beyond my control. I had to wait, help where I could and simply accept the situation. When the accident occurred, the only thing that mattered was the well-being of Greg and his partner Keri. Getting him to safety was our first priority. The expedition was the least of our concerns and it had to be put on hold until Greg was stabilized. While in the Falkland Islands, it did not matter how many perfectly suitable sailors, skippers and crewmembers we found who were willing to take Greg's place. Keri had first to agree to continue with the expedition with a replacement crewmember. And secondly, she had to agree upon the suitability of the crewmember.

During the time when I started working on Plan B, to paddle around the Falklands, it was the process that made me feel back in control. I felt a lift in my mood and a surge in my motivation. I was already in the Falklands, the islands I was planning to kayak around and it required no need for a support vessel. All I needed was a kayak, charts, and away I could go by myself. During that time, there was a small part of me that wished for Plan B to actually get implemented. I was thoroughly enjoying the thought of freedom and independence. But when Brian came along and Keri agreed to continue with the expedition, my dream was rekindled. The absolute joy that my dream could still become a reality overtook any desire to kayak around the Falklands. Yet, at the same time I recognized that the control and freedom I thought I was getting close to were once again lost.

In many ways it did not matter how late we were leaving Stanley to get to South Georgia; nature took care of when and how comfortably we would arrive. During the journey, I discovered that I had more patience when nature was in control, rather than another person. During the crossing, in the middle of the South Atlantic, while I lay in my bunk, the carbon monoxide alarm sounded. I felt uneasy. There we were in house-sized waves, being thumped about by the wind, land at least four days away, and our only means of shelter and transportation was the boat that was potentially under threat.

My uneasiness stemmed from not knowing what was going on and why the alarm had sounded. I did not have an understanding of the systems onboard. I suddenly wanted to know every detail of what caused the alarm to go off, wanted to check all possible leakages myself. Keri and Magnus, familiar with the workings of the *Northanger*, were fairly relaxed and figured it was the old diesel heater that had not been used for some time and was now burning off the dust that had accumulated. I never slept a wink that night; I lay awake constantly sniffing the air.

When we finally arrived at South Georgia, I felt a sense of relief, albeit fleeting. Much to my disappointment, Keri decided to anchor one day's sail away from Grytviken. She did not want to run the rest of the way at night; a gale force wind was supposed to pick up sometime in the next twenty-four hours. We were so close to my starting line and I desperately wanted to be reunited with my kayak.

Our three-week delay in arriving left me only two weeks to accomplish what I had set out to do. The odds looked hopeless. It was time for me to be captain of my own boat and start taking back the control of the expedition.

Keri and I have had a difference of opinion numerous times. I had never before come across a controlling person like her, and I felt like a child arguing against her own parent. We each had a job to do and we each had our own way of doing it. I felt that in any team it is important to let each member have control of a specific task, one that they can call their own and take pride in having accomplished it without assistance. Keri didn't see it that way. It seemed that she watched, controlled and criticized every move we made.

I recognized the challenges Keri faced every day. Being in charge of a vessel in South Georgia is no easy feat. I admired her strength in actually having had the courage to continue this journey without Greg. It was her skills and willingness, although at times reluctant, that got us here. I recognized her limitations and the limitations of simply sailing in South Georgia. At times I felt she jeopardized the expedition but, by the same token, she gave us the opportunity we needed.

March 10th

The latest discussion onboard this morning with the crew has finally got some facts straightened and out in the open. Keri has often blamed Beth-Anne and my flight commitments for the shortage of time for the expedition to be completed. Well, when we all sat down I said, "OK, let's push the flights back then, let's forget about them and get this mission accomplished." Suddenly there was a change of heart. Both Magnus and Keri expressed their need to be back no later than April 3rd. Keri then said, "So we can't have you going around to the west coast. It could be days away before we could actually get weather to allow us to go around and pick you up." She wants us to be ready to leave by March 12 or 13. My stomach does flips at the thought.

Chapter 24

End of a Dream

The next morning I woke to calm and peaceful paddling conditions. Eager to be on the water, I rose early and packed quickly. It was an easy launch as the surf hitting the beach was not even two feet high and the beach was steep, enabling me to get snug in my boat on dry land, secure my sprayskirt and launch onto the welcoming sea. After the first few paddle strokes my body felt strong and my mind clear. It was going to be a good day. Today I will make some miles, perhaps even get as far as the north tip. That idea excited me and spurred me along.

My body felt comfortable sitting in a seat it now knew well. My paddling stroke was smooth and in rhythm with the water as I navigated my kayak over glassy swell. The complexity of this rugged coastline, the boomers and erratics that appeared spontaneously, made me feel relieved that I had waited to do this section today. Had I paddled it in the horrific conditions yesterday, it would have been dangerous.

I knew the *Northanger* was anchored in Right Whale Bay. Once I arrived at the mouth of the bay, I pulled out my handheld radio and gave them a call. This was one of the few times that we were actually in radio range. I opted for a quick way to let them know my plan and destination for the day.

"Northanger, solo sea kayaker," I called.

"Go ahead solo sea kayaker, *Northanger* here." It was Keri who answered.

"Hi Keri, I'm aiming for Elsehul today. I have great conditions and the forecast looks good, over."

"Hayley, we have to pick you up and make our away back to Prince Olav. There is a huge storm coming and I don't want to be in Elsehul for it. It's not safe. We don't have the time or weather to continue any further north, it is time to turn back."

On this rare calm day with a forecast favourable to make many miles, I was pulled off the water. I felt devastated. I understood our limitations and, as a mariner myself, I could absorb the big picture. I knew it was the best option, but I resented it just the same. This was the moment when I shifted from being in denial to coming to terms with the stark reality that I would not complete my kayak expedition around South Georgia Island.

I suddenly had an urge for this recent radio call to be rewound like a video cassette, as though it had not taken place. I wanted to be back feeling strong and excited about the possibility of paddling north with the intention of rounding the northern tip in these more than ideal conditions. But alas, I am no video cassette and I cannot run away from the sequence of events that just led to the termination of my expedition.

As I paddled across Right Whale Bay I thought about continuing on anyway, despite Keri's unwillingness to go further. I could make my own way to Elsehul with or without the *Northanger* and wait out the storm. But then what? Keep going and hope for perfect weather? Being stuck on the southwest side leading into a sub-Antarctic winter could lead to an unintended lengthy stay in South Georgia, including a long and restless winter. We simply had run out of time to round the northern point and continue down the southwest side. The *Northanger* and her crew had commitments elsewhere; Beth-Anne had a job to get home to, and we had flights to catch. Prior to this day, we attempted delaying our flights, just to give me a little more time; however, the earthquake in Chile had taken that option off the table.

While the *Northanger* lifted anchor in preparation for its rendezvous with me at the mouth of Right Whale Bay, I sat drifting on the pleasantly calm sea. This was the first time since the beginning of the expedition that I had nowhere to go, with no pressure urging me on. I did not paddle. I just simply sat and observed my surroundings. All the other times on the water I had needed to continuously paddle, otherwise strong winds and currents would have taken me backwards – not to mention the many miles I was always trying to make up for. However, at this moment I rose and fell with the movement of swell while penguins porpoised beneath and around my floating boat. Seals drifted in to join the marine parade as did as a black-browed albatross that glided silently overhead. I glanced towards the north wishing I was paddling in that very direction. That coast will remain a mystery, just like how the mountains are continuously cloaked in clouds, their peaks shrouded in mist. The southwest coast of South Georgia remains untouched by me and unseen by my eyes, for now anyway.

As we sat at anchor in Prince Olav Harbour waiting in anticipation for the storm to arrive, a feeling of urgency swept over me. I wanted to be camped onshore, among the animals and the elements which had become my home. As I sat within the confines of the *Northanger*, with her thick steel hull separating me from the outside world, I felt deprived of South Georgia. With only small, unopened portholes to look out from, the elements seemed banished from my existence. 'I might as well be back in my cottage in Alert Bay,' I thought. The belligerent calls from whining seals, and the grumbles and grunts of lethargic elephant seals were muffled by the steel walls that separated me from my South Georgia. I did not want to remain on the *Northanger*.

Chapter 25

My Final Day in South Georgia

A heavy easterly system did arrive and rearranged the features of what was once a calm bay. We arrived in benign conditions and, only twelve hours later, the water now seethed with whitecaps and the tussock grass on the surrounding hills lay at ninety degrees, bending in the breeze.

During the two days we sat waiting for the storm to pass I concocted a plan. Having watched carefully the weather forecasts as they came in, and after calculating the miles ahead on our southerly journey, it seemed clear that I could actually camp another two nights and kayak for at least one more day. The weather looked good for the following day. The *Northanger* runs at six knots; we have forty-eight miles to get to Grytviken; we could be in Ocean Harbour which is just fifteen miles past Grytviken by 4:00 pm tomorrow afternoon. It is a safe place for the *Northanger* to anchor in the light winds that are forecasted and I could then paddle the fifteen nautical miles heading north, enter East Cumberland Sound and camp really close to Grytviken on the last night. This meant that the following morning I would only be a thirty minute paddle away from Grytviken and kayaking in sheltered waters for a mere three miles. Even the forecast was on our side. This would give me an entire day to clean, pack and prepare for the following day of departure. Perfect. Now let us see what Keri thinks of this plan.

Well, as usual she completely rejected the idea because it was not her idea. She did not appreciate that I had taken the initiative, tried to gain a handle on a situation and come up with a reasonable plan. She had every excuse under the sun to say that it would not work. It was a well thought out plan; there was no reason it could not be done and there were no risks being taken which would jeopardize the safety of the boat or crew. I reacted strongly to her denial and my words were probably tinged with some sarcasm.

"That's it!" Keri shouted. "We are going straight back to Grytviken, this expedition is over!"

"You can't hold me captive on your boat, Keri," was my reply, and then we both stormed off towards the confines of our cabin.

That evening I apologized to the crew for bringing frustration and anger onto the boat. I apologized to Keri for my comments and she agreed that my plan was sound. Ocean Harbour was the next day's destination.

I spent the entire day outside, on watch, observing the coastline I had paddled along the last ten days. The upper coast was masked in clouds and the summits were saturated in mist. As we entered Ocean Harbour the sounds of animals gave evidence that it was teeming with life. No sooner had the *Northanger* dropped anchor than I was packed and ready to go ashore and be immersed in South Georgia and my expedition once again. It was a damp evening but this did not dull my spirits. As I went about the chores of setting up my tent and cooking my evening meal, I felt a great respite. This afternoon while approaching the shore, I saw the largest elephant seal of all time. He surfaced like a submarine only a foot away from my kayak as I drifted towards shore. It scared the crap out of me. It expanded its trunk as though showing me who's the boss. This amazing specimen kept me awake all of the night. Can you imagine the sounds that came out of that giant?

I thought the morning would offer hours of reflection as I paddled in calm conditions, pondering, soul searching and not having to concentrate too hard. It was completely the opposite. South Georgia does not allow you to have a single day off. Today ended up being the most difficult paddle day of all, yet there was very little wind to speak of.

As I set off the sun was peaking though the clouds. It was gorgeous as it rose from the base of the sea, sending beams of light across the entire bay. 'It would be a placid day on the water,' I thought. As I approached the entrance of the bay, kelp beds and reefs dulled the breaking swell and confused the rebounding water. I had to give them a wide berth and give up the idea of paddling on the inside. The motion of the swell beneath my hull lifted me up then steered me down on every wave that passed. Oh, that's right; we just had two days of stormy weather. The ocean is bound to be unsettled as it recovers, only to prepare itself for another building system.

Having rounded the head at the entrance of Ocean Harbour and now on the outside coast, I could see that the swell out here was at least three metres in height. It charged from the northwest towards the shore, throwing itself against the cliffs and returning confused and kerfuffled. My kayak was being shoved this way and that, and for the next four hours it would be a wild ride. I could not take my hands off my paddle. Every stroke assisted as a support stroke. I was forced to keep a close watch on every wave and how it responded to the movements of my kayak. I literally had to prepare myself and boat for every wave I summited. Rock by rock, bay by bay I made my way along the coast, at times travelling nearly two miles offshore. The inside passage, between the island and reefs, although more picturesque, was not an option today. The large swell caused the waters on the inside to be unruly and unpredictable as waves, which on a calm day would have been benign, spontaneously exploded over hidden rocks and reefs. It was a treacherous gauntlet that promised only to lead to carnage.

Black-browed albatross kept me company most of the morning. In my attempt to capture the intensity of the conditions and the occasional reflection I was able to offer, I had my mounted camera filming for most of the day. I felt edgy, concerned by the superstition that something bad was bound to happen on my final day. I did not feel very stable in my boat, regretting the choice of design for a moment. Not wanting to take my hands off the paddle, I could only sip water and take a quick bite of my energy bars occasionally. Andrew McAuley's sad story came to mind. He was only 50–80 km away from the coast of New Zealand after having paddled across the Tasman Sea from Australia. He would have been the first to complete this mission. All that was found was his kayak; he left a wife and young child behind. These thoughts plagued me. Most accidents occur on the way down from a mountain, when guards are down and bodies are tired.

After paddling for four and a half hours nonstop, South Georgia put on a grand appearance. It was as though the curtains were parted and the main show was about to begin. The clouds lifted revealing craggy peaks that pierced the cobalt sky. Icebergs lit up like lanterns and the seas were touched by the sun and glistened beautifully. As I turned into Cumberland Sound, the swell eased and I could relax my hands from my paddle. I took advantage of this reprieve and guzzled water and ate three energy bars. The final hour took me deeper into Cumberland Sound and nearer to Grytviken, my finish line. I embraced the rhythm of me moving freely on the glimmering sea as I selected a landing site for my final night camping in South Georgia.

Chapter 26

Back with Shack

It seemed rather fitting to be in rain and drizzle on my final day paddling in South Georgia. It couldn't help but dampen my spirits as I reluctantly paddled into Grytviken. The summits dissolved into the sky and mist crouched heavily upon the mountain peaks. I felt low on energy and lacked enthusiasm as I paddled lazily towards the shore. 'Perhaps I should stop in and visit a 'friend' before heading to the *Northanger*,' I thought. I headed directly to where Sir Ernest Shackleton rests.

The bleak conditions made no difference to the feisty characters that loitered on the beach. There is always a liberal gathering at this particular landing site. I recalled one time having difficulty landing onshore with passengers keen to visit Shackleton's gravesite. The dense populations of critters who assemble here like security guards at a rock concert simply take up all of the room, leaving very little for a zodiac to land and passengers to step onshore.

As I plodded up the trail in my soggy sandals a feeling of nostalgia overwhelmed me. I felt so disappointed that I was arriving at Shackleton's grave with a mission unaccomplished and a dream unfulfilled. My expedition was incomplete. It was a failed attempt. I was returning to Canada without triumph and deeply indebted to the bank.

I weaved my way between the numerous crosses that stood between the gate and Shackleton's grave and knelt by his granite headstone. I have never felt as subdued as I felt that day. With the camera running, I chatted with Shackleton, expressing some of what I was feeling. I glanced about the scene that surrounded us. Here we were, alongside the whaling station of Grytviken. We had a few things in common, Shackleton and I. We were both drawn to this island because of our fathomless adventurous spirits. We followed our passions, acted on our dreams and tried our best to make them come true. Although his expedition's challenges were far grander and more extreme than any of what I had experienced, we both managed them in similar ways. He faced each obstacle in his stride, calmly and thoughtfully, always moving forward and seldom looking back. He never gave up and just kept on trying, as though each setback was part of the plan. He did not succeed with what he set out to do but his achievements were far greater. His leadership, strength and wisdom led his men during unbelievably trying times and brought each and every one of them, under his charge, back home safe and alive after a two-year ordeal. Because of this, his story is far richer, more profound and moving, more so than it would have been if everything had gone as planned. Do the best stories really derive from failed expeditions and Plan B's? It would seem a true adventure is essentially a measure of what is experienced?

If I had completed my circumnavigation of South Georgia, I know right now I'd be feeling fantastic, proud and fulfilled. But things did not work out that way. I too have an adventure story to tell. In success, the lessons I might have learned might possibly be less intense than those I gathered on my journey, my pilgrimage as it were.

"I'm going to turn this adventure into something big," I announced out loud to the granite gravestone. I had an incredible adventure. My dream was to kayak solo around South Georgia Island to raise awareness for the albatross, an endangered species. Did I succeed?

Well, I kayaked alone around parts of South Georgia – *Check*. I camped alone around parts of South Georgia – *Check*. I had thousands of people following my track and blog and they were made aware of what is happening to the albatross – *Check*. Have I a story to tell, a film to make and a book to write? *I think I do*. Did I inspire others to follow their dreams, despite impossible setbacks? *I think I did.* I did it all, minus a few miles and a section of coastline!

> *It seems as if everything thus far has brought nothing but delays and challenges.*
>
> *So what are we to glean from all of this; the regular clichés of patience, perseverance? You may not be able to perceive the greater lessons or the bigger picture until some time has passed. This could be a lesson in, "despite your greatest efforts in life, some things just don't pan out the way we want them to". I'm not really sure what this is all about, or what to say. I'm just happy for you, for being able to have at least felt with your five senses, or more, your dream! It didn't go down the way you had envisioned, but you gave it your best and most noble attempt. Hayls, I am proud of you and what you have accomplished, I'm proud of the way you have conducted yourself in the face of huge disappointments. I'm proud of you for your determination and grit. In my eyes (and many others) you have conquered so much more than just a physical island, heck, at this point...South Georgia is a mere technicality! You have endured the crashing waves of disappointment, the fierce winds of change, and the rocky outcrops of compromise. You have successfully completed the South Georgia of the mind and spirit. Hayley...you have encompassed the true essence and spirit of your hero Shackleton and you did it with just as much grace and integrity. That in itself is a journey like no other.*
>
> -An email from Dean to Hayley

These words from Dean helped me at this time.

I picked myself up from the ground, grabbed my drenched tripod and camera and made my way towards the kayak. A juvenile elephant seal slumped alongside the trail and objected to my passing. I gave it a wide berth and thanked him for sharing his South Georgia. Once settled in my cockpit, ready to paddle the final one-hundred-metre stretch, I took a deep breath, held my face towards the rain and enjoyed the tiny droplets that fell on my face. 'I am absolutely the luckiest person alive,' I thought. Look what I have seen and where I have been and all the experiences I now have stored in my memory – memories that will endure a lifetime. With that final thought, I began to paddle towards the waiting crew on-board the *Northanger*. Perhaps I'll be just in time for a hot breakfast and a hot cup of tea.

Chapter 27

Going Home in Luxury

A devastating earthquake with an 8.8 magnitude occurred in Chile on February 27th. It was the strongest earthquake ever recorded at the time, causing at least four hundred deaths. I felt for all the innocent people who suffered and were now left with their world literally turned upside down. How peculiar that something so far away, on another continent, could affect others who are simply trying to circumnavigate an Island by kayak. We were only faced with the task of finding new flights from a new destination and, due to my rather tight budget, this was not a straightforward chore. I booked my original flights using the frequent-flyer miles which I had collected over a three-year period. This was the only way I could afford flights for myself and Beth-Anne, but this really limited the possibilities of flight changes. Back in Victoria, our friend Sally had dedicated much time, energy and patience trying to get new flights since the Santiago airport was closed. She called twice a day for over two weeks, hoping for a cancellation which we could then snap up. One of her many calls met with success, as two flights came open; the international flights were leaving from Buenos Aires. That was to be our next challenge.

I had to find a way to get us and our gear to Buenos Aires. Getting there from Ushuaia was our best option. The *Northanger* however, was not an option. If traveling on the *Northanger*, we would have to wait for a decent ten-day weather window to journey back across the Drake Passage. Once in the Falklands, Keri and Magnus had plans to spend at least a week there before continuing on to Ushuaia which would be another seven-day crossing. We would well and truly miss our flights.

Just out of curiosity and with a tiny fragment of hope, I looked at the expedition ship schedule. By mid-March, with deteriorating weather, ships are generally finished for the season and are on their way to northern latitudes. I noticed that one ship was due to arrive in Grytviken on March 17th. I couldn't believe our luck. This was perfect. The *Prince Albert II* could be our ticket to Ushuaia. Now all we need is a willing captain to take two passengers, two kayaks and a bundle of bags. 'Oh please give us a ride,' I wished.

I had one thing on my side; I was very much involved in the Antarctic tourism industry and a respected expedition leader. I decided to write directly to the EL onboard as well as to the captain. I wrote a brief summary about the expedition and the events leading up to our need for a ride. I offered to do presentations onboard for the passengers about the expedition, emphasizing the point that they would be the very first to see it. This ride to Ushuaia would be our only hope. I remained anxious until receiving a reply. It came quickly and it bore good news. We were welcome onboard the three-star *Prince Albert II* bound for Ushuaia.

Sally cancelled our flights from the Falklands to Santiago and rebooked them departing from Ushuaia and bound for Buenos Aries. The ship would get us to Ushuaia with a few extra days up our sleeve to indulge in *empanadas*, a pastry deliciously stuffed with cheese and vegetables or spiced meat, inexpensive but delicious wine and plenty of relaxation.

Beth-Anne was ecstatic, probably more relieved than anything. She suffered terribly from seasickness while on the *Northanger*, even when the boat was anchored in a calm bay, and her six foot seven frame was simply too cramped on a confined sail boat. Lying in a bunk for several days and nights can't be that good for you. Sailing back on the *Northanger* could have been fatal! Well not quite, but I believe she had suffered enough.

My good news is not yet over. Because of the particularly nasty forecasts over the last three weeks (the whole time I have been trying to kayak around South Georgia), the *Prince Albert II's* schedule was rearranged; but it was in our favour. Instead of heading from Ushuaia to the Falklands, then on to South Georgia, finally finishing up in the Antarctic Peninsula, they decided to go straight to the Peninsula from Ushuaia, then on to South Georgia and finish their voyage with the Falkland Islands as a grand finale before making their way back to Ushuaia.

What does this mean for us? Let me explain.

1. We get to spend another day in South Georgia, landing at two primo landing sites – Salisbury Plain and Prion Island – yes, nesting wandering albatross again!
2. We then get to spend two days in the Falklands – one in Stanley where I can drop off the borrowed kayak and store *Banana Split* at a friend's house. The other day will be spent at the two most fabulously divine black-browed albatross nesting colonies – filming opportunities galore and adventures still to come.

Things could not get any better. This allowed us to spend another day in South Georgia as well, and a chance to say goodbye on better terms.

Saying farewell to the dedicated crew aboard the *Northanger*, having been connected at the hip as we shared tough times and fun times together, was as surreal as boarding the *Prince Albert II*. At the top of the gangway, we were met by an elegantly dressed woman in a skirt, nylons and high heeled shoes, who guided us to the spiral staircase that led to the owner's suite on the sixth floor. This would be our cabin for the duration of the journey. Dressed in fleece pants and Gore-Tex jackets, carrying our bulging bags and kayak paddles, we trudged through the lush carpeted corridors, supporting ourselves using the polished brass banisters as we climbed the coiled staircase. Upon entering the cabin I had to pinch myself for the extreme change in our environment. From a tent to a luxurious cabin made up of three rooms, three beds with dressing gowns and sequined slippers placed neatly alongside. The 'lounge' had a flat-screen TV, a fridge filled with chocolate, champagne and beer, and the marbled bathroom had a four person bath in it with jets. It was all a tad overwhelming. What do we do with all of this stuff and how on earth did we score the owners suite?

That evening, as we each held a complimentary gin and tonic (with ice and lemon), the expedition leader introduced us to the other passengers. They had already been onboard for two weeks so new faces would be somewhat obvious and required an explanation, especially those dressed in fleece rather than gowns. He spoke briefly of our reasons for being onboard and made mention that we may not be dressed as per the usual dining room dress code. We were made welcome and admired our first of many five-course meals which looked too beautiful and artistic to eat. Despite the lack of elephant seal grunts and whimpers from fur seals, that first night on board, I slept like a baby.

The day we landed on Prion with the passengers from *Prince Albert II* offered conditions fairly different to what Beth-Anne and I had experienced a week ago. On this day, the wind tampered with the inside waters which we had to cross in our zodiacs to make a landing. Whitecaps collided with the wind, sending salt spray towards those who sat on the windward side of the boat. As we approached the beach the resident fur seals scrambled down to greet us, showing no fear of our convoy of zodiacs. Once ashore, passengers in small groups took turns making their way to the top of the island via a newly built boardwalk which minimized our impact on the tussock grass and creek.

Like a tropical hula skirt the tussock grass shuffled vigorously, rustling in the twenty-knot breeze and shimmering in the sunlight. Throughout the day the wind continued and the Wanderers made full use of the wind. Giant birds soared above, at times fairly close to where we stood. We observed them walking awkwardly towards the steep edge of the island and then plucking up the courage to take off, perhaps for the first time. Like an infant taking its first step, the newly fledged albatross flapped their eleven-foot wings in the vast and open sky in preparation for taking their first flight. Once aloft, they are immediately transformed into graceful flyers as though they were repeating a familiar act. There were some juveniles who were not yet fully fledged, the occasional patch of down still positioned amongst their fledging feathers. They flapped their wings while standing on the nest, training their muscles and preparing for their big debut.

I counted at least four courting albatross pairs in various areas on the tussocks, each involved in a unique performance in the hope of out-dancing and impressing the other. At the highest point of the island, where the boardwalk ends, I sat watching an adult who sat upon a solid clay-like nest. I was five metres away from the albatross. As I filmed, I observed every detail; its broad soft-pink beak with the distinctive nostrils that secrete salt. Their eyes are beady black but distinctive with a ridge-like brow that gives an albatross a stern and serious expression. I marvelled as it unfolded the massive twelve-foot wings, joint by joint like an elasticated tent pole. At one stage I noticed the bird becoming agitated. It fidgeted on the nest, as though it was no longer comfortable, like a dog on a tangled mat that needed to change position. Finally it stood up, revealing the hidden treasure that perhaps was the cause of the discomfort. A newly fledged chick, only a few days old, sat within the secure caverns of the parent's brooding pouch. It had hopes for being fed as it bobbed its little head upright, aiming for the parent's beak. The chick was a bundle of white fluffy down and for fifteen glorious minutes we watched with pleasure the unfolding drama of new life.

By the end of our time onshore most passengers had returned to the ship. A handful of people, including myself and Beth-Anne, remained. We had been there for six hours and we still had not experienced enough. The golden hour was upon us and my reluctance to leave was as strong as the angelic light that glazed over the mountainous land of South Georgia. The sea was awash with an amber tinge as the descending sun stained the frisky whitecaps that governed the waters. Icebergs drifted silently, merging within the horizon, glowing like sapphires. Pristine mountains, sharp in contrast, gave us a full view of every summit that soared up to the sky and the Wanderers kept company with the peaks. The scene was intoxicating and I could not help but surrender to this moment.

The time had come to say farewell to South Georgia and it was at a time when the island was presenting its most favourable side. Unrest entered my thoughts. I was uncertain when I would return to South Georgia and this troubled me. It filled me with sadness, as though leaving a lover forever whom I was still madly in love with. I wept with gratitude and joy, thankful and relieved that I was long ago led to this place. It has stolen my heart, turned my world around and made me feel more alive than any other place I know. Up to my final minute ashore, I indulged in the luxury of this remote land, knowing that I would be back.

Epilogue

As the lights dimmed in the Centennial Theatre, I made my way towards the podium and glanced out towards the audience. Over two hundred faces stared back at me, awaiting my presentation. It was February 15th, 2011 and I was the evening speaker for the Vancouver International Mountain Film Festival. I looked behind me at the screen, expecting my first slide to appear; but the screen remained dark, void of light and image. The equipment technician called out from the back of the theatre, "There is a technical glitch and it may take a minute or two."

I decided to use this opportunity to give a little background as to where I just flew in from. I spoke of my first experience shovelling snow while living in Ontario this past winter, adding the detail that I went door to door, offering to clear other driveways for a small fee. "A writer has to make a living somehow," I announced in jest. "For eighteen years I have lived in Canada, yet I've never had the opportunity to shovel a single driveway. I finally feel like a true Canadian."

For seven minutes I improvised, building a relationship with the audience and warming them up for the real presentation. By the time the technical glitch had been resolved and I began my presentation, my nerves had vanished. I am certain that since having returned from South Georgia, very little seems to faze me. I was more than happy to be up on stage during this exciting evening.

While I spent the summer piecing together a number of presentations to take to the road, Dean took on another creative endeavor. He carved a wandering albatross out of western red cedar. It was life-sized and we called it *Arnie*. He too was part of the cross-Canada presentation tour.

Our presentation tour began October 3rd, 2010. I rented out my cottage and moved into a newly purchased 1979 Winnebago with Dean. We named our new wheels, *Winnie*. With *Arnie* tied to the roof and our belongings securely stowed, we boarded the 3:15 pm ferry and departed the shores of Alert Bay. It was the beginning of our cross-Canada presentation tour and we were bound for Lake Shawnigan, the venue for my first of many presentations.

Two thirds of the way there, the journey took on similar characteristics as the South Georgia expedition. With a fan belt missing and an overheated radiator, we sat parked along the shoulder of the Trans-Canada Highway, experiencing what would be the first of many breakdowns during our travels across Canada. We dealt with the situation calmly. Dean worked on the mechanical problem and I figured out how I could make it to the presentation on time. It was the first time I had hitchhiked to a presentation but I did not know then that it would not be the last.

As we journeyed through the provinces of Alberta, Saskatchewan and into Manitoba, Dean and I established a new dimension in our relationship. One dark and rainy evening as we drove along the Kokahala highway in B.C., trucks sped past us as though they were entered into the Indy 500. We travelled at the conservative speed of 90 km per hour. Suddenly the wipers slowed to a stop, the headlights dimmed then shut off completely and our engine failed. All power in our motorhome had ceased to exist. With the little momentum the motorhome still had, we glided into the shoulder that was as wide as a dining room table for four. It would not do for our thirty-foot motorhome but there was no other choice. We were in sheer darkness and silence; even our hazard lights were not working. We were an accident waiting to happen as trucks sped past our invisible presence.

I ran outside and placed a flashlight on our stern and began lighting all our candles inside. Once we were visible to passing traffic, I walked along the edge of the highway with my cell phone held above my head in an attempt to get cell phone reception. We had joined the BCAA[22] the day before.

Dean jumped into MacGyver[23] mode to try and figure out what had happened to our power. In the midst of this burst of activity, we both acknowledged that there was a possibility we might get rear-ended by a speeding truck. If that was the case we felt we needed to say *the* words (with no apologies for the cliché): "I love you Dean"; "I love you too Hayls." We continued trying to resolve the problem. Moments later, miracle worker Dean got the engine started but we were uncertain how long it would stay running. It seemed our fan belt was not charging the alternator. Once under way, and both of us preferring to drive in daylight hours, we pulled into the first rest area we found and spent the night.

A plugged fuel system, two flat tires and a new alternator later, we rolled into Winnipeg only minutes away from parking our motor home for six weeks while we worked a contract in Churchill, Manitoba. As Dean maneuvered from one lane into another, he accidently clipped a vehicle that was passing on the inside lane. Dean moved in behind the car he clipped and stopped, got out and met up with the driver, both of them eager to inspect the damage. The guy was surprisingly calm and not in the least bit concerned about the tiny nick that appeared on the rear right side of his vehicle. I stepped out to join them and made my way to the guy whose car we had just clipped, my arms open ready to give him a hug. Dean was dumbfounded when he realized that I knew the guy. Dean had just clipped the only person I knew in Winnipeg.

The journey thus far brought out new strengths, or perhaps ones we had yet to discover, for Dean and me, as individuals, and as a team. Our varying skills, attitude and ability to problem solve complimented the other's. Without realizing it, we discovered a mutual compatibility.

---

[22]British Columbia Automobile Association

[23]MacGyver is an American action-adventure television series created by Lee David Zlotoff and Henry Winkler.

After our work in Churchill, Manitoba, was complete, which included me giving at least three presentations, it was time to take to the road and continue the presentation circuit. We were bound for Ontario. Dean was a little apprehensive as we climbed back in the saddles of *Winnie,* anticipating breakdowns, knowing that this time we would be fixing and mending in cold and snowy conditions. Despite the blizzards we drove through and the chilly mornings, we were forced to pull ourselves out of bed and into a cold cabin.

We arrived in Niagara Falls free of any vehicle problems. Perhaps the curse was broken. Although the main reason for our visit was to spend Christmas and New Years with Dean's family, a presentation was arranged at the Niagara Falls Nature Club's Christmas meeting. The club had a strong birders component and they were appreciative of my presentation. But *Arnie* the albatross was the main attraction. He soared on stage at waist level, able to look folks in the eye as they sat listening to my presentation.

This one presentation led to a dozen more, and so our intended one-month stay extended into five months. Dean found work cooking at a restaurant overlooking Niagara Falls and I visited numerous school, clubs and colleges bringing to life the world of the albatross, the concerns as to their status and my adventures around South Georgia. The presentations were geared around letting people know not only the threats the albatross and other seabirds face due to human impact but also to offer simple solutions as to how an individual can make a difference.

This presentation tour was self-propelled. The phone never rang off the hook for bookings, nor did my sponsors host any events. I had to work just as hard to create an interest for speaking engagements. I needed to promote the expedition, the adventure and the cause all over again.

Most people embraced the adventure story that told of the struggle against unexpected odds. I was happy to find that most audiences and readers of my published pieces seemed receptive to the story which portrayed the very essence of life: *Things don't always go as planned no matter how meticulous your planning is.* That is why the mechanical breakdowns and the occasional technical difficulties did not bother me during the presentation tour.

Was this expedition a success or failure? It really depends on how I look at it.

As I sit here, after many hours staring at a computer screen, I envisioned where I was a year ago today, April 6th 2011, exactly a year since I returned from paddling in South Georgia. The time has flown. As I moved through the process of writing this book and doing many presentations, I have relived my South Georgia expedition all over again. How perspectives can change over time and emotions tempered.

I recall my emotional entanglement with the expedition and sometimes I feel embarrassed about how passionately and sensitively I reacted. I hear that Keri and Greg are doing well, continuing with their charters, spending much of their time adventuring down in Antarctica and even back in South Georgia. Greg can still play the cello and is adapting to new techniques when using his power tools. Keri continues to make the best carrot cakes in the whole wide world.

Soon after the expedition, Magnus sailed his father's boat back to New Zealand from Punta Arenas. It was his first open ocean crossing as captain. He had friends aboard but neither of them had very much sailing experience. He was twenty-one years old on the expedition but at times he seemed to have the wisdom of a forty-year-old.

Brian and Lin finished their contract in the Falklands and were eager to head back to Malaysia. They sailed in the neighboring Malaysian waters, visited family in England and recently put their boat the *Stormwitch* up for sale. They have decided to give up their life under sail and take up residence on land, for now anyway. As I have gone through the process of writing this book, I turned to Brian frequently, asking him to recall certain events, wanting to make sure I was accurate with my facts. I look forward to the day when I see Lin and Brian again.

Beth-Anne returned to Victoria B.C. and dove into a busy year of guiding and teaching.

As for the albatross –

Ken Passfield has lived in the Falklands for twenty years. Having heard about our unexpected arrival he came down to the boat to visit Greg and Keri whom he had not seen for thirteen years. Although Greg and Keri were at the hospital, we invited him onboard for a cup of tea. Our conversation soon turned to South Georgia. He had only just returned from spending three weeks there, counting wandering albatross and their nests on Prion and Albatross Island. Unfortunately, he did not come bearing good news. The numbers of nests and breeding pairs over the past few years had dropped considerably, reaching an all-time low with this recent count.

Since the mid 1950s the Falkland Island government has supported annual bird surveys on the chain of islands adjacent to South Georgia, where the largest flying bird in the world, the wandering albatross nests. Bird biologist Sally Poncet has been involved with this South Georgia project for twelve years and, during her involvement, breeding pairs of wandering albatross have dropped from one hundred and eighty to one hundred and twenty nine pairs. There is every indication that the cause of this steady decline is the longline fishing industry in the waters off the Brazilian and Uruguayan coast. Unfortunately these efficient flying birds cover thousands of miles during their extensive foraging flights. They fly out of their 'home' zone where new longline fishing methods and equipment have been implemented, to zones where numerous international longline fishing fleets are still using out-of-date techniques, and therefore are accidentally catching and killing albatross. The birds are also exposed to the illegal longline fishing industry.

Some countries involved in the commercial fishing industry have gone through some radical changes over the past twenty years. Catching the most fish in the least amount of time was the goal of the past. Today, however, conservation and management issues are changing the industry's focus. Meeting conservation goals and adopting sustainable harvesting practices now take precedence over increasing harvest. According to a University of Rhode Island gear specialist, "technology is already too efficient at harvesting." Today's gear must reduce the incidental capture of nonmarketable species. Innovative longliners are meeting this goal by modifying vessels, fishing methods and gear to concentrate on target species and to eliminate by-catch.

Looking at South Georgia as an example, this particular fishing zone has seen a drop in the incidence of seabirds being inadvertently drowned on longline hooks while taking the bait. How was this accomplished? By following CCAMLR (Commission for the Conservation of Antarctic Marine Living Resources) and government conservation measures such as fishing at night, weighting lines so they sink immediately on entering the water, deploying streamers and discharging offal on the side opposite to the vessel's longline deployment.

The Government of South Georgia has received international recognition for its sustainable management of the marine environment. The Marine Stewardship Council has certified the South Georgia toothfish fishery, commending the government's achievements in conserving the valuable stock and in protecting the related ecosystem. Very few fisheries in the world achieve this status. Such results are possible worldwide if we can continue informing the public and raising funds to implement positive change.

It is fishermen that are becoming the innovators, coming up with new techniques and equipment that work not only to eliminate by-catch but help the fishermen get their job done. New Zealand, Australia and South Georgia are leading this conservation effort. Because of the limitless range of many seabirds, particularly albatrosses and petrels, a coordinated effort between countries is essential to safeguard their future. Besides, the countries that are implementing changes in the industry require coordinating the work of governments, agencies and individuals around the world to spread the 'seabird smart' word.

There is a program called the Albatross Task Force consisting of a team of people braving the high seas to spread the word of these simple solutions. They work in the world's by-catch hotspots of Southern Africa and South America where albatrosses come into contact with large and diverse longline and trawl fishing fleets, where albatrosses are most in danger. Task Force members individually explain safer fishing methods to fishermen and ships' captains, encouraging them to use these solutions onboard their vessels. The Task Force also works onshore, running workshops with fishermen and fisheries management bodies, and carries out research to identify solutions that best suit each fishery. Dramatic results can be achieved by people working with fishermen. The Albatross Task Force introduces the albatross to fishermen, presenting a simple understanding of the animal, its cycles and vulnerability.

The broader public also has a responsibility, and choices, about the food we buy and the entrées we order in restaurants. Our choices of fish could make a difference to species of bird life, let alone fish, and perhaps even save them from extinction.

Where there is a vision of hope, there is chance of survival. As the Albatross soars in the winds of the Southern Ocean, let the spirit of our hope soar as free as the wind, reaching all expanses of our world and touching many people. May the albatross fly in our skies forever.

Selected Bibliography

Books

Caroline Alexander, *The Endurance*. Alfred A.Knopf, New York, 1998

Tim and Pauline Carr, *Antarctic Oasis, Under the Spell of South Georgia*. W.W. Norton: New York, 1998

Tui De Roy, Mark Jones, Julian Fitter, *Albatross, their world, their ways*. Christopher Helm: London, 2008.

Carl Safina, *The Eye of the Albatross: Visions of Hope and Survival*. Henry Holt & Company: New York, 2002

Graham Charles, Mark Jones, Marcus Waters, *The Unclaimed Coast: The first kayak journey around Shackleton's South Georgia*. Penguin Books Ltd: London, 2007.

Articles

Frances Kinslow, *The Effects of Pelagic Longlining on PA*. A journal of Academic Writing, Volume 4, Number 1, HOHONU – University of Hawaii at Hilo Hawaii Community College, 2006

I would like to thank all those involved in the South Georgia Expedition

Special thanks to:

Beth-Anne Masselink
Brian and Lin Cartwright
the *Northanger* crew – Keri Pashuk, Greg Landreth and Magnus O'Grady
the King Edward Point Research Station staff
Jonathan Selby
Gerald Hartwig
Paul Friesen and Beth Dunlop
dear friends in Ushuaia – Alicia Petiet, Ana and Fernanda
Sally Eshuys
Win and Kal Laar
Larry St Pierre and Kathy Rall
Hayley's friends for their support
the Wild Places Fund
Karel Doruyter
Adventure Philosophy – Graham Charles, Marcus Waters and Mark Jones
Quark Expeditions

With much appreciation to:

All you kind folk who made a donation
All the blog followers; your support and encouragement really helped

Much gratitude to the following Falkland Islanders:

Sally Poncet   Janice Dent
Ken Passfield   Steve Dent
Chris Clarke   the Royal Air Force Mount Pleasant

Thank you to my Expedition Sponsors:

Necky Kayaks   Gore-Tex

Kokatat Watersports   Polar Sea Adventures POLAR SEA

Werner Paddles 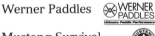   Frontiers North Adventures

Mustang Survival   Knight Inlet Lodge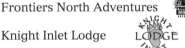

Ingle Insurance **INGLE** INTERNATIONAL

Harvest Foodworks    Sky Eye and Xaxero with
                                                Global Marine Networks www.xaxero.com

Rasdex Kayaking Clothing

Thanks to Ashis Gupta with Bayeux Arts for showing an interest in my book idea, for your patience and friendly approach to publishing.

Thanks to Michael Richardson for connecting us together.

Sincere gratitude to my family – I love you all so much:

Val Thomas, John and Fran Shephard, and Naomi Shephard

I could not have done it without you and I love you:

Dean Laar